LORI PECKHAM editor

Guide's Greatest

HERO STORIES

PATHFINDER • JUNIOR
BOOK CLUB

D1522934

REVIEW AND HERALD® PUBLISHING ASSOCIATION
Since 1861 | www.reviewandherald.com

Published by Review and Herald® Publishing Association, Hagerstown, MD 21741-1119

This book was
Edited by Lori Peckham
Designed by Emily Ford
Cover art by Marcus Mashburn
Typeset: Goudy 13/16

PRINTED IN U.S.A.

16   15   14   13   12   5   4   3   2   1

Library of Congress Cataloging-in-Publication Data
Guide's greatest hero stories / Lori Peckham, editor.
      p. cm.
1. Christian biography—Juvenile literature.   I. Peckham, Lori. II. Title:
Guide's greatest hero stories.
  BR1704.G85 2012
  277.3'0830922—dc23

                                        2011038288

ISBN 978-0-8280-2637-6

Contents

Dedicated to . . .

Lori Turpel Diaz and Erin Stuart-Cayot, who befriended me when I was the new kid in fourth grade who had moved to California from New Jersey and said "water" with a weird accent.

Michelle Brumagin Bergmann, Marissa Smith, and Jackie Ordelheide Smith, who are great friends and great moms, which makes them heroes in my book!

Special Thanks to . . .

Randy Fishell, *Guide* editor, and Rachel Whitaker, *Guide* associate editor, for their wonderful recommendations for this volume—and for being good heroes to lots of kids.

Tonya Ball, desktop technician, for her speedy preparation of this manuscript and her dependability in contacting authors.

Anyone who is a hero to someone—whether for showing attention, kindness, courage, or love.

Jesus, our ultimate and eternal hero, who gives each of us an invitation to live a heroic life like His.

"Two people are better off than one, for they can help each other succeed. If one person falls, the other can reach out and help. But someone who falls alone is in real trouble" (Ecclesiastes 4:9, 10, NLT).

Also by Lori Peckham:
   Guide's Greatest Animal Stories
   Guide's Greatest Grace Stories
   Guide's Greatest Mission Stories
   Guide's Greatest Mystery Stories
   Guide's Greatest Narrow Escape Stories
   Guide's Greatest Rescue Stories
   Insight Presents More Unforgettable Stories
   Jesus in My Shoes

To order, call 1-800-765-6955.
Visit us at **www.reviewandherald.com** for information on other Review and Herald® products.

A special thanks to the authors we were unable to locate. If anyone can provide knowledge of their current mailing address, please relay this information to Lori Peckham, in care of the Review and Herald® Publishing Association.

Prayer in the Blizzard

by Clarice Stoneman Widman

I doubt that any of the children in our class regarded Anna as anything but a freak before the day of the blizzard. She seemed almost like a friendly puppy, following us around the schoolyard, anxious to please but always doing the wrong thing. Everybody laughed at her awkward mistakes.

Anna was from a German refugee family that had come to the United States to live. She was tall for her age and very slender, with thick braids the color of clover honey, shy blue eyes, and a smile that quirked only one corner of her wide mouth.

Anna could not speak English—that was the reason she seemed always to be doing the wrong thing. Our teacher, Miss Bailey, put her in our class because she was just our age: 12 years old.

Miss Bailey asked us to include Anna in our

games, but since she could not understand us any more than we could understand her, she was often left out. Miss Bailey frequently kept her after school to teach her "picture" words.

That's what Anna was doing one November afternoon when Paul and Fred Jones, Alberta Sloan, and I started home. It was one of those warm Indian summer afternoons, too warm for November even in Kansas, where the autumn days linger sometimes well into December.

"It's such a wonderful day," said Alberta. "Why don't we go out to the Gringhams' black walnut grove and gather some nuts? Mr. Gringham said I could gather nuts in his grove anytime I wanted to. It would be fun."

"I could stop at Uncle Jack's feed store and get some sacks," offered Paul.

"Mother likes the flavor of black walnuts." I added my bit. "I can surprise her with some nuts for the fruitcake she's going to bake tomorrow."

"We'd better not." Fred shook his head. "We're expected home right after school. Why can't we plan to go tomorrow?"

"Because it might be stormy tomorrow," said Alberta. "The weather forecaster says a storm is coming over the weekend."

"It looks very much like it!" scoffed Paul, rolling his head in all directions to view the cloudless sky. "I wouldn't be at all surprised if we'd be snowballing each other at this time tomorrow!"

We all laughed. The idea seemed ridiculous.

"Come on; I'm going," said Alberta, firmly walking away toward the country highway.

We all hurried to catch up with her. Even Fred forgot his objections and crossed the road to help Paul get the sacks from his uncle's feed store.

We followed the road to a small creek at the edge of town, then cut across an alfalfa field, skirted a large hay barn, and walked on through a woodlot. Beyond a large pasture of buffalo grass we could see the trees. It was farther than I had imagined. I had never been on a hike that had taken me so far from home before, and I liked the excitement of the adventure.

Just as we reached the grove we looked back and saw a girl in the distance. She seemed to be following us.

"It's that German girl, Anna," Paul said. "She helps Mrs. Gringham with the housework on weekends. I suppose she'll be coming over here, tagging after us."

But Anna didn't come by the grove. She just waved to us from the pasture and continued on her way.

We didn't work very hard at gathering nuts. We found it great fun to pelt each other with the balls. The husks were soft and cushioned the sting of the direct hits.

Suddenly we noticed that the sun was not shining so brightly anymore. Gusty blasts of wind sent the dry leaves whirling high into the air. It was getting cold. Gray clouds rolled across the sky.

"If we're going to fill these bags before dark, we'll have to hurry," said Fred.

We stopped our playing and began to gather nuts as fast as we could.

Finally Alberta said, "I'm going home. I'm cold."

"Yes, let's all go home," I said. "We have plenty of nuts anyway—all we can carry." I didn't have to persuade anyone else. They were all ready to go, and soon we were hurrying across the pasture toward town.

We hadn't gone far when Paul said, "Look, it's beginning to snow."

Then suddenly there were many, many flakes whirling and swirling about us. It was getting colder by the minute, and our light summer clothing was little protection against the raw wind. And we had to face that wind. Fred led the way, and we followed single file behind him, getting some small protection from the worst of the blasts. The distance across the pasture seemed endless. We could see only a few feet ahead. The storm seemed to surround us on all sides like a white wall.

"I'm cold," said Alberta, beginning to cry. I felt like crying too.

"We should have reached the woodlot long before this," said Paul. "It will be better when we get into the shelter of the trees."

"There's a dark object ahead of us," said Fred, wiping the crust of snow from his face. "Perhaps it's one of Mr. Gringham's cows." Then suddenly Fred shouted, "It's Anna!"

Sure enough, it was Anna, with her arms full of warm clothing she had borrowed from Mrs. Gringham. She knew we had no coats with us and were not prepared for the sudden storm.

We joked and laughed as Anna helped us put on the warm coats. Even Alberta wiped away her tears and seemed cheerful again.

Then we started on. Anna took Fred's arm and motioned that we should follow her.

"But she's going in the wrong direction," objected Paul. "We don't want to go to the Gringhams'. We want to go home."

The boys carried on an argument with Anna in sign language for what seemed like hours, but was really only minutes. Finally Anna gave up and nodded her head to show them that we must follow her. It was beginning to get dark, and the snow was still falling thickly about us.

On and on we went. The storm seemed to be fiercer than ever. We gave up trying to talk to each other because it took all our breath to struggle forward against the wind and snow. Even the warm coats were not enough protection against the icy blasts.

Alberta began to cry again. "I'm cold," she

whimpered. "My feet feel like clubs. I know they must be frozen. We're going to freeze to death out here in the storm."

I had been fearing the same thing secretly. Maybe we would never reach home again. By unspoken consent we had all left our nuts by the wayside.

Then suddenly we bumped smack into the side of a building. It was the hay barn. We had wandered from our course enough to miss the woodlot completely, but luckily we had not missed the barn as well. We followed the boys around the building. Fred opened the door, and we hurried inside.

It was dark and cold in the barn, but the protection was a welcome rest from our battle with the storm. We stood close together in the snowy darkness. From the dim light that entered the doorway I could see that Anna was moving some armfuls of hay into a corner. Then she pushed us all toward the comfortable place she had prepared. We sat in a circle on the hay, resting.

The hay smelled musty and damp, and before long we felt even colder than when we had been out in the storm. Alberta was still crying.

"Stop that sniffling," said Paul. "What are you crying about anyway? We aren't lost. Just as soon as we have rested up we'll go on home."

"Sure," said Fred. "We'll be home soon—then we'll catch it! We shouldn't have gone to gather nuts without permission. We were expected to go straight home from school with no dillydallying."

"We're sorry," I said, "but that doesn't help us now."

"I'll never do this again," wailed Alberta.

"Nor I," said Paul. "We've been very foolish."

Then we all sat silently, waiting for someone to make the first move to start out into the storm again. No one did. The patch of gray light that was the doorway grew darker. The wind whistled about the eaves. I could feel the snow sifting in on my face, but I was too cold and miserable to care.

It seemed like hours later that I suddenly awoke. What had awakened me? Then I heard it clearly. It was a voice—Anna's voice. She was talking in German, and I could not understand a word she was saying. Yet somehow from the tone of her voice I knew that she was praying.

I was stiff with cold, but I stumbled to my feet and found my way through the darkness to her side. As she continued her prayer I found myself repeating it after her: "Unser Vater in dem Himmel . . . Dein Reich komme . . ."

Anna's prayer gave us both the strength we needed. We roused the others, and all together we marched back and forth across the narrow cleared space. Anna began to sing one of the hymns Miss Bailey had been teaching us for the Christmas program, "It Came Upon the Midnight Clear." We all joined in, and it seemed almost as though we were back in the schoolroom again. We forgot for the moment that we were cold and hungry and far from home.

Just as we finished singing the second stanza we heard shouts outside the barn. We ran to the door. The lights from Mr. Gringham's big truck shone into our faces.

An hour later five cold, tired, and hungry children were delivered, by way of the Gringham truck, to their worried parents.

From that day on Anna was one of us. We helped her to learn our language and took turns staying after school to drill her in "picture" words.

"Miss Bailey," said Alberta one day as we were helping our teacher after school, "when we were lost in the blizzard Anna said a very beautiful prayer in German. Jesus heard Anna's prayer and sent help to us. Do you suppose we could get Anna to teach the prayer to us?"

That is how it happened that our whole class learned to say the Lord's Prayer in German. Ever since then those words have reminded us that Jesus is always near at hand to hear a prayer—in any language.

2

"Nothing Exciting Ever Happens"

by Ellen E. Morrison

Connie stepped from the front door onto the porch in time to wave to her friend Alice, who was speeding by on her bicycle. Then she sat down on the stoop, looking very lonely, and feeling lonely too.

"This is such a quiet town," she said to herself. "Nothing exciting ever happens here. If I had a bicycle, I could at least go places in the afternoons the way Alice does."

But Connie knew that it would be a long time before she would be able to get a bicycle. Mother and Dad couldn't afford to buy one now, and Connie had to spend her babysitting money for other things she needed.

She watched the new yellow daffodils nodding beside the front walk. A stray breeze blew her hair over her face, and as she brushed the strands back she thought how pleasant the breeze felt on this unusu-ally warm day in March.

Just then her mother came to the front door and said, "Connie, please go over to Mrs. Brown's and ask her for the cake recipe she promised to give me."

"Sure, Mother," Connie replied, glad to have something to do. She knew Mrs. Brown quite well, for she often stayed with her 3-year-old daughter, Shirley.

The Brown home was only a block away, and Connie reached it in a few minutes. As she walked up to the front door, Mrs. Brown called to her from a neighbor's house. "Go right on in, Connie. I'll be there in a little while, as soon as I make a phone call. My telephone is out of order."

Connie decided to sit on the front porch instead of going inside and settled herself in the swing. She wondered where Shirley was but then remembered that the little girl was probably up in her room taking her afternoon nap. Yet suddenly she thought she heard Shirley's voice. It sounded as though she were outdoors somewhere.

Connie left the swing and walked to the front steps. She heard Shirley distinctly this time calling "Mommy!" in a voice that sounded afraid. Again it came: "Mommy!"

The call seemed to be coming from high up. Connie moved down the steps and away from the house so she could see Shirley's upstairs bedroom window. It was open about six inches, and Shirley had her hands on the sill and her face at the opening, crying. Suddenly terrified, Connie realized why the child was afraid. Smoke was seeping out of the window on both sides of Shirley's head!

"I'm coming!" Connie gasped, her voice hardly more than a whisper. She ran into the house and up the single flight of stairs to the second floor. There she met flames pouring from a hall closet. Shirley's room lay beyond. How could she reach the child?

Then she noticed that there was a space about two feet wide between the opposite wall and the flames. She ran to it and paused a moment, until another faint cry from Shirley spurred her on. Pressing close to the wall, she crept safely past.

Through the smoke she saw that the door to Shirley's room was open. She ran in and found the sobbing child still at the window. "Shirley!" she cried, overjoyed at finding her unharmed. Afraid to lose a moment, she picked up the child and started back into the hall. The smoke had become so dense by this time that it set them both to coughing and brought tears to their smarting eyes.

Connie strained to see through the smoke. Could it be possible? Flames had blocked their way of escape!

Still carrying Shirley, Connie ran back into the bedroom. She threw the window open wide and saw that several people were already running toward the house, Mrs. Brown among them. From somewhere off in the distance a fire siren wailed.

But Connie knew that she could not wait for help. Frantically her eyes scaled the side of the house. They came to rest on a drainpipe, scarcely a foot from the window.

With quick presence of mind she hurried back to the bed and stood Shirley on it. "Get on my back, Shirley, like you do when we play horse!" she exclaimed, turning around so the little girl could obey her command. Flames were already licking at the threshold of the door.

Shirley climbed on her back. "What are you going to do?" she asked in a tiny, childish voice as Connie carried her to the window.

"I can't tell you now," Connie answered, trying to sound calm, "but just hold on real tight!"

Carefully Connie stepped up on the windowsill, not daring to look to the ground below. With two swift kicks she discarded the black patent-leather pumps from her feet. She reached out for the drainpipe and clutched it with both hands. "Hold tight!" she repeated to Shirley. But she didn't need to. The little girl was holding on for her very life. Connie took her feet from the windowsill.

Frightened gasps arose from the crowd below.

For a brief moment Connie tested the drainpipe,

hoping against hope that it would hold this extra weight. It gave slightly, but showed no other signs of weakening. Slowly she began to go down. Above them red tongues of flame, mingled with smoke, appeared at the window.

Below, all eyes were turned upward, watching the two girls. Even the arrival of the fire engines did not divert their attention. When Connie at last set foot on the ground, a loud cheer went up from the watchers, who crowded around to congratulate her.

Mrs. Brown, eyes filled with tears of relief and happiness, clasped Shirley close in her arms and said to Connie, "I am so grateful to you. I don't know what we would have done without you!"

A voice arose from the midst of the crowd. "What do you say we raise another cheer for the bravest girl in town?" The crowd responded with a hearty shout that made Connie blush.

The next afternoon, when Connie came home from school, she saw the delivery truck from Johnson's hardware store parked in front of her house. The deliveryman was removing a shiny new bicycle from it. Connie walked up to him and exclaimed, "Don't you have the wrong address?"

"I don't think so," the man replied, a twinkle in his eyes. "Aren't you Miss Connie Danford?"

"Yes, I am," Connie said, surprised.

"Well, then, this is for you!" By now the bicycle

was out of the truck and sitting on the front walk.

Connie, breathless with excitement, noticed an envelope bearing her name tied to the handlebar. Quickly she tore open the flap and removed the note inside. It read:

Dear Connie,

We could never really repay you for your bravery in saving Shirley yesterday. Your mother told me once how much you want a bicycle, so we hope you will accept this one as a thank-you gift from us.

With love and deep gratitude,

Mrs. Janice Brown

Connie refolded the note and tucked it in her pocket. With unbelieving hands she caressed the shiny handlebars, murmuring happily, "And I was the one who said that nothing exciting ever happens in this town!"

Day the Sheep Came Through

as told to Lilith Sanford Rushing

Anytime now the sheep herds will come through," Papa announced one spring morning at breakfast. "Seeing the sheep men and their dogs drive the herds through town on their way to market will be something you'll never forget."

His eyes turned my way. "Jenny, aren't you excited?"

No, I wasn't. I had a heavy burden in my heart. It had been there ever since Lora French had joined our school about six weeks before.

"Jenny's always grouchy these days," complained my older brother, Joey. "She won't even play catch with me anymore."

I felt my mother's eyes on me, and I looked down at my plate. I had told her about the worry gnawing inside me.

That Lora French! Her cruel tongue was as painful

as a beesting! She would join me every morning on the way to school, and then my humiliation would begin.

Lora was the prettiest girl in our school. She was about a year and a half older than the rest of us, but she was always pale and headachy and could never take part in the strenuous games. For some reason she detested me. And because Lora was popular, the other girls shunned me too.

We finished breakfast, and I dressed for school. As my mother braided my hair, she said, "I know it's hard, but ask God to help you. He never fails! And Jenny, did you ever ask yourself whether you might be doing something to make Lora treat you the way she does? You know the Bible says, 'Do good to those who hate you, . . . pray for those who mistreat you.' Turn the other cheek."

"Oh, Mother, I've tried and tried! I can't understand why she torments me. I've never done a bad thing to her."

"Come on, Jenny. We'll be late!" came my brother's voice.

"I wish I didn't have to go," I said weakly.

But soon I was on the way to school. Near the big bridge that spanned the Concho River, Lora and her brother, Grant, joined us. Then Joey and Grant left to go to the junior high school.

The moment we started walking across the long bridge, Lora's tongue lashed out. "You ugly country girl, with all your freckles and your skinny legs, what do you think you'll learn at school today?" Her blue eyes blazed.

I struggled to say something in reply, but I could not. I had freckles and long, wiry legs, and I knew it.

"Why don't you speak up?" Lora went on. "You're as awkward as a kangaroo!" She began walking briskly across the bridge.

The bridge had a wooden ledge about a foot wide running the length of it near the height of my shoulders. When I had first met Lora, I had climbed onto this ledge and walked along it, showing her how brave and strong I was. Was this where her hatred for me had begun?

We finally arrived at school, and Miss Woolworth began our geography lesson. But my mind wouldn't settle on the lesson. I suddenly remembered that the merchants in town had been putting away the boxes of produce they usually set out on the sidewalk for display. Did that mean the sheep were coming through? Would I miss the excitement?

"Jenny Price, why are you sitting there daydreaming? In what country is Calcutta?" Miss Woolworth's voice startled me.

I stammered, "Calcutta? Why, it's in Russia."

Everyone laughed. I sank low in my seat, flooded with humiliation. Lora leaned across the aisle and whispered loudly, "Numskull! Dumbbell!"

I wanted to cry, but I couldn't. Then the devil must have moved in my being. I began to plot a way to get back at Lora. How could I hurt her as much as she had hurt me? I cast aside all the wise words our Bible has for our conduct. I forgot that I had one Friend even when all the world was against me.

I revived somewhat when the teacher said, "Jenny, please go to the blackboard and work out this example in division. You are the only pupil who seems to understand how to divide fractions."

But at recess my misery returned tenfold. I don't know how Lora ever managed it, but I found that she had written the word "kangaroo" in large letters on the back of my white blouse. The others laughed as if their sides would split.

After crying awhile in the library behind a bookrack, I took off the blouse and turned it inside out. It looked odd, but it was better than it had been.

The rest of the day the other students were dying to laugh at my funny-looking blouse, but they dared not do it in the schoolroom. The only thing that kept me from despair was my new determination: I was going to get even with Lora French.

School let out early, and in the hurry I lost sight of Lora. Going down the crowded schoolhouse stairs, I noticed the amusement in the eyes of my classmates.

"You won't find Lora," a tall boy told me. "She was feeling sick and hurried home."

I glared at him and went on. Then I remembered that there was a big stick lying near the edge of the playground. I snatched it up and ran to the street. I would beat Lora's legs and arms! I would hit her hard all over her body! I would pull out most of that beautiful hair!

I took a shortcut to the bridge, knowing that Lora had to cross it. As I ran past a store, a man standing in front said to me, "Little girl, get out of the street! The sheep are coming through! You'll be trampled!"

"They won't trample a tall girl like her!" someone replied.

I rushed on but suddenly paused. The sheep! They had probably entered the outskirts of town already! And when the herds got to the bridge, would Lora be there? Lora, with her pale face and weak body?

I dropped the stick. Lora would be helpless, frightened like a kitten! I wasn't afraid for myself; I was strong enough to jump out of the way and run, but not Lora!

"Dear God," I tried to pray. "Dear God, forgive me for letting myself be taken over by evil! Why did I do it? Please forgive me."

I began to run as I had never run before. Voices called after me, telling me to get out of the streets, but I didn't heed them.

Finally the bridge loomed before me. I ran onto it, straining my eyes for Lora.

I could hear the short-clipped barking of sheepdogs. Was that thick thudding the sound of sheep walking onto the bridge? Yes! I could see the gray horde at the other end.

Where was Lora? Finally I spotted her—a small knot huddled against the railing near the center. I raced on, screaming till I thought my lungs would burst. "Lora, climb! Climb to the ledge!" The little bundle didn't move.

I reached her where she half squatted, a frozen ball of fear. "Climb to the ledge!" I cried. "Reach high and put your hands on the support rods."

She made no move. I snatched at her hands, placed them on a steel rod, and began pushing, lifting Lora up. She revived a bit and helped herself at last.

After some panicky moments I got her onto the ledge and quickly pulled myself up after her. I held her there by placing my arms on the rods with Lora between them.

The sheep were now crowding over the floor of the bridge. There were stout old rams that might have harmed Lora when they found her in their path. There were others that could have trampled her.

As the sheep passed below us, hardly six feet away, I felt Lora's body relaxing. She began to cry. "Oh, Jenny," she sobbed, "I've been so mean to you. So very, very mean!"

"Just look at the sheep, Lora," I said. "We'll never have as good a chance to see them go through as we have this minute!"

But Lora kept on. "Jenny, I'm so sorry! The day you climbed up to this ledge and I knew I couldn't, I was jealous. And when you were so strong and so good in games and so smart in math, I couldn't stand it! I was sick two long years and couldn't play. I got behind my class; I failed twice in math. I hated you, Jenny! But I don't now. Please, please, can you understand?"

"Yes, Lora," I said. "I understand." I felt light and happy again.

Lora said, "Jenny, we can be friends, can't we?"

"Yes, yes," I said, "we can. But look at the sheep! Don't look on this other side down to the water, though."

The water was deep and dark down there, but I wasn't afraid to look at it. I had just conquered water so much deeper, so much darker and more dangerous, that ordinary water could not frighten me.

4

Lucy and the Light

by Kay Heistand

By now Lucy was so worried that she could hardly keep from crying.

She sat down on a large rock by the shore to watch for her father. The waves splashed higher and higher as the sun began to set and the shadows lengthened. Lucy had a right to worry, for her father was the lighthouse keeper, and he had never before been away from his duty at night.

Lucy and her father lived on a small, rocky island where a tall lighthouse guarded that part of the Atlantic coast. In her father's hands rested the responsibility of keeping the lamp lighted to warn the great ships to steer clear of dangerous rocks.

This day, as he had done many times before, Father had taken his small boat and gone to the mainland to buy supplies. Dusk was now creeping in, and still there was no sign of him. A wind had sprung up, and waves roared against the rocks, as if trying to catch Lucy's feet. She moved back a little and strained her eyes to see over the white foam.

Lucy had always been a timid child. She had no friends, for she led a very lonely life on the little island. Books kept her company, and her father and her religion were her beacons.

As the daylight faded Lucy knelt and prayed for God to tell her what she ought to do. Should she light the lamp? When she rose to her feet, she felt filled with courage. Her heart was eased, and she knew what she must do.

Going into the lighthouse, she lighted a candle. Taking a long taper and matches, she began to climb the steep, winding stairs. But Lucy had a secret problem—she was terribly afraid of heights. Imagine! A lighthouse keeper's daughter who feared high places!

Lucy had tried very hard to overcome this fear, and she didn't think her father had even guessed it. On this lonely, stormy night it took a lot of courage to climb those steep stairs alone. But up she went.

She tried to shield the flickering candle with her body. (This was long before everyone had electric lights.) Grasping the cold metal railing tightly, she climbed as quickly as she could, not once daring to look down into the depths below.

Reaching the platform at the top of the tower, she

studied the large light for a moment. She had watched her father light it many times, but she had never done it by herself.

It was almost dark now, and the wind was raging in a fury. Angry waves pounded against the lighthouse so that it trembled.

With a deep breath, Lucy lighted the long taper. Standing on tiptoe, she lighted all the big burners. A prayer for help slipped between her lips as she adjusted the valves and waited for the pressure to build up. Then, as the large lantern flared into life—bright and clear and glowing, flashing out for miles across the ocean—she cried with all her heart, "Thank You, God!" And her cheeks were wet with tears of tension and relief.

All that night Lucy waited. Her worry over her father's absence and her fear that the light might fail kept her awake.

When at dawn the fury of the wind and the waves subsided, Lucy took up her watch on the shore again. There at last was Father's small boat coming through the gray mists!

She ran into her father's arms as soon as he beached the boat.

"Thank God, my child, that you lighted the lamp!" he cried, stroking her fair hair.

"What happened, Father? Are you hurt or ill?" She hugged him tightly.

"Two men stopped me at my boat yesterday afternoon. They detained me by force so I couldn't get home to light the lamp. They kept me a prisoner in a small shed. They belong to a gang that planned to rob ships that would be wrecked on the rocky coast when there was no light to warn them off. But when the men saw the light come on, they knew that their plan had failed. They let me go. But I didn't dare to cross the rough water in the night. Oh, Lucy, I'm so proud of you!"

"I was worried and frightened, Father. And I could never have done it alone." Lucy brushed back her hair from her forehead. She stood tall and straight, and the shadows of the night's fear were gone from her eyes.

"Not done it alone?" her father exclaimed, his eyes searching the shore. "Who was with you?"

"My God is the rock of my refuge,"* Lucy quoted softly. "His hand guided me, His strength gave me strength, and His presence cast out all my fear."

Father looked at his daughter, and there was a gentle benediction in his eyes. "We are never alone. It makes me very happy to see that you have learned this great truth."

---

*Psalm 94:22, KJV

5

"Flavoring" Pete

by Lilith Sanford Rushing

Sandy Myers always smelled like ripe peaches when he came home from work in the late evening. His mother didn't mind the peach smell, but she disapproved of Pete Burns, the boy whom Sandy rode to work with.

"Mother," Sandy said one morning as he waited to be picked up, "I wish you wouldn't worry about Pete. He got me the job, and I appreciate it. Jobs for teenagers have been really scarce this summer. I sure like working in Flood's Orchard, especially during peach season."

Flood's Orchard was about eight miles outside the city limits. It was one of the biggest orchards in the state, and now the finest peaches were ripe enough for harvesting.

As Sandy stepped on the porch to listen for Pete's

noisy old car, his mother joined him. Her face was bright and cheery.

"Son," she said, placing a hand on Sandy's shoulder, "I shouldn't be concerned about Pete's influencing you for bad. You can influence him for good, instead. Your influence can win out over his."

"Oh?" Sandy said. He didn't quite understand.

Mrs. Myers laughed. "Well, you should be like an onion or a banana. When either of them is put in the refrigerator without a covering, the other foods take in the flavor. I remember one time when all our butter tasted like bananas."

"I get it, Mom. I'll try to 'flavor' Pete for good!"

Pete's car roared up to the curb at that moment, so Sandy told his mother goodbye. Riding along with Pete, he tried to think of how to influence his friend for good. *It's not going to be easy,* he thought, as Pete drove past another car, almost crowded it off the road, and gave a mean laugh.

They reached the big orchard with its hundreds of acres of fruit trees. The sun was warm, and a strong aroma of ripening fruit filled the air. A buzz of activity had already surrounded the long building where the fruit was sold. And long flatbed trailers pulled by tractors were rolling out toward the heart of the orchard. On board each of them were a driver, a helper, and a buyer.

It was Sandy and Pete's job to be useful wherever

they were needed most. Sandy ran to a trailer whose driver beckoned him. He noticed that Pete got on the one just behind.

On both sides of the narrow road were trees loaded with fruit in varying stages of maturity. Bees were humming everywhere, and yellow wasps were making a feast of the fallen fruit. Soon the tractors stopped, letting the riders off. Pete and Sandy picked the fruit and lifted the heavy baskets to the trailers. Sandy noticed that Pete wasted a lot of time kidding around with the children who'd come with their parents. As Sandy worked, he almost despaired of influencing Pete at all, for if he lectured him about neglecting his duties, Pete would surely resent it.

Later in the morning Sandy and Pete were asked to work at the main buildings. This was the hardest part of their job. When the peaches were checked out and paid for, Sandy and Pete lifted the filled baskets from the trailers and put them in the customers' cars. Such work brought on aching backs after a while.

Sandy had been doing his job quickly and politely, placing the fruit carefully in the cars just as he was directed. He lost track of Pete's whereabouts.

As loaded trucks began pulling in from the orchard, Sandy was told by his boss to work at the checkout center.

A small distance from the office building was a long, barnlike shed in the midst of a grove of willow trees. This building had wide tables in it, and here the seconds of each day's harvest were put. These were the windfalls, or inferior peaches. Mrs. Flood, the owner, had told Pete and Sandy never to sell any of these seconds. Sandy often wondered what happened to them. Each morning when he came to work he'd see this place empty; yet as the day went by, more and more inferior fruit would fill the tables. By the next morning it would be gone again. Where did it go?

As Sandy turned from lifting two baskets into a car parked near the seconds shed, he saw a strange thing. Pete loaded one of the baskets of seconds into a car and put the money for it into his own pocket. It all happened in a rather sly way.

Sandy just stood speechless. He knew that no helper or truck driver was supposed to handle any cash transaction at all. This was an office worker's job. Sandy wondered what to do, what to say. Did he have the courage to try to "flavor" Pete for the good?

A truck driver who hadn't been far away approached Pete and Sandy, an odd look on his face. "Boys, you'd better get back to work now! This isn't your rest period." He turned and went back to his truck.

Pete hurried to his work, but Sandy thought miserably, *I've failed to use my influence.*

Later in the day both boys were assigned to the orchard again. Sandy longed to say, "Pete, how could you sell those seconds and put the money in your own pocket? Were you given permission?" But every time he was near Pete, he didn't have the courage.

In the middle of the afternoon the climax came. Sandy observed that Pete was edging his way to the shed where tables were now filled with baskets of inferior fruit. He'd seen Pete talking in low tones to certain customers.

Sandy thought he heard Pete saying, "If you want a bargain, you can really get it here with the seconds." And when a purchase was made, Pete put the money in his pocket, looking about furtively to be sure he hadn't been spotted. Sick at heart, Sandy knew he couldn't keep still any longer. He went over to Pete.

"Pete, what are you doing? You're not supposed to sell any fruit. And I saw you pocket the money." Sandy felt his voice trembling, but he had gotten the words out.

"Sandy, mind your own business!" Pete fumed. "This stuff is just taken out and given to hogs! Hogs, mind you! Why shouldn't I make a little extra?"

Sandy was just about to answer him when Mrs. Flood stepped out from the other side of the shed and stopped in front of them. She was a slim, dark-haired woman with a kindly face; she wore a serious expression, though, and her voice was stern when she spoke. Her eyes were on Pete.

"Your name is Pete Burns, isn't it? One of my drivers told me you were selling this fruit. You've been doing a dishonest thing. Please go to the office immediately and get your pay—and don't come back."

Pete began to stammer out how he thought it wasn't such a bad thing to make a little money on the fruit since it was just taken out and given to hogs.

Mrs. Flood replied, "It's true that the man from the hog farm takes a small amount that is impossible to use for anything else, but most of this fruit goes to charity places, to homes for the elderly, to orphanages, to churches, where it is canned and put up for people who can't take care of themselves. The workers in these places sometimes stay up the whole night canning, or making jams and preserves and jellies. So, young man, you were stealing from them! And I want you out of here at once."

Sandy knew the moment had come for him to be courageous. His voice and his knees were both unsteady, but he did manage to speak. "Mrs. Flood, please let Pete stay. I've wanted to influence him for good. My mother said it was what I should do. But I haven't had the nerve to say anything till now. Pete needs work so much. His mother is a widow, and he has little brothers and sisters. After this, if you'll keep him on, I'll see that he doesn't sell any more of the fruit. I'll try hard to help him do what is right!"

He stopped short, and his eyes fell before Mrs. Flood's intense gaze. Had he been too bold, too outspoken?

Pete came to his side and put a hand on his shoulder. His face was red with shame, and he took the money from his pocket and placed it on one of the tables. His voice came thick and slow. "Mrs. Flood, I—I've done wrong. But I know better now; I won't do it anymore. I want to be more like Sandy. Please give me another chance, Mrs. Flood."

Pete was humble now and repentant. Mrs. Flood's face lost its sternness. She said almost cheerfully, "Pete, I'll let you come back, but I want Sandy to look after you, as he says he will. Remember, in honesty there aren't any seconds." Turning to Sandy, she said, "You are a true friend."

After Mrs. Flood walked away, Pete smiled at Sandy gratefully. "Thanks for going out of your way to help me. I really do want to change my ways."

Sandy grinned, giving Pete an encouraging slap on the back. *Boy, have I got some news for Mom,* he thought, *and I think she'll like the "flavor" of it!*

6

Marcia's Magic Violin

by Fannie A. Smith

"It isn't much fun to practice," Marcia said as she put her violin in its case. "What good does it do anyway? No one cares to listen to me playing. The other children are running around having a good time outside, and I have to come in after school every day and just practice."

Marcia didn't realize that she was talking out loud. Mother came in just then and said, "Are you through practicing for today, dear? You really are getting your piece well! How much can you play by memory now?"

"I played it all today several times and some yesterday. Do you think I'll have it for the recital, Mother? It's only a little over three weeks away."

"Oh, yes, it sounded very good today—much improved."

Marcia felt better after that and said, "You'll help me when you can, won't you? I want it perfect!"

"Yes, of course. We'll begin really working on it tomorrow. It is the prettiest piece you've had, and I enjoy accompanying you on the piano. Now you may rest until supper time, or go out and play with the children."

Marcia ran happily across the street to play with Dorothy, her best friend, who was trying out her new croquet set.

School and practicing kept Marcia busy all the next week. Soon it was lesson day again, and that meant a trip to Hollywood to her teacher's studio. Mr. Curtis, the teacher, had telephoned to say that a crew was working on one of the main roads near Hollywood, and there would be several miles of detour. Knowing this, Mother and Marcia started early and hoped they would reach the studio on time.

When they came to the detour, they saw that there was a bad traffic jam. Working people were going home at that hour, and as Marcia and her mother drove along, the jam got worse and worse. Sometimes they didn't move for 10 minutes or so, and then only a very little bit.

Nearly everyone was getting irritable and impatient. Horns honked all around them, on left and right, in front and back. The noise only made the situation more stressful.

Mother said, "If they would only be more patient, it would be so much better."

"Mother," Marcia said thoughtfully, "haven't I heard

somewhere that there's magic in music and that some-times it calms people when they're angry and upset?"

"Yes, I've heard that too, and I believe it does," Mother replied.

Marcia was all excited. She had just thought of something. "Do you suppose there could be any magic in my violin, if I played something? Do you think any-one would listen? Shall I try it? What shall I play?"

While she was taking the violin out of the case and waiting for the next stopping place, she said, "I believe I can play all of the mazurka by memory now, and it would give me good practice for the recital. Do you think I dare?"

"Yes, dear, it would be very nice if you did. Forget yourself and think only of your violin and how pleased the people will be. We can ask the Lord to help us when we're doing something that will help others and please Him."

Marcia always had a hard time playing in public and felt shaky and scared, but she tuned her violin carefully, and when there was another stop in the traffic, Mother opened the door.

Marcia stepped out beside the car. She had just room enough to stand and draw her bow across the strings.

All was noise and confusion, but she began her piece with long sweeping bows, as her teacher had taught her. Windows and car doors opened wide, and people leaned out as far as they could. Frowns turned to smiles.

The girl's nimble fingers flew. Sometimes her bow was bouncing and her long, blond curls bounced too. Her lips were slightly parted in a smile, and her eyes and cheeks were all aglow with excitement. She made a charming picture.

She felt glad now that she had practiced her scales, and the different kinds of bowings seemed easy; it was fun, now that she could do it right.

She played as she had never played before.

The happy faces all around her were thanks enough. When she finished there was a hearty burst of applause from the cars around her. The people clapped and waved and called, "Thank you, thank you." She smiled and bowed and waved back. They were still waving and smiling as they turned off the detour onto the highway again.

"Oh," Marcia said breathlessly, "that was fun, Mother, and I wasn't a bit scared. I believe they liked it, and it wasn't hard at all. I'm glad I practiced it so it's easy now."

In the years that followed, Marcia became a good violinist and was glad she had practiced when she was young. She found that people loved to hear her play, especially at programs at church, school, and rest homes.

She remembered her teacher's advice to forget herself and use her talent to bring pleasure to others. And she never forgot the time when, at the age of 11, she played for a large and appreciative audience on the detour road to Hollywood.

7

Salani and the Bush Baby

by Helen Dizney

Salani was the newest picker at the African tea estate. He was 12 years old, and by reaching he could pick the tender leaves at the very top of the tea bushes. These were the best of all the leaves and were separated from the rest.

He stepped off the path to reach for a clump of leaves high on a bush. There was a stabbing pain in his leg. A snake had struck. Salani fell to the ground, crying with the terrible pain. The snake slid quickly back into the shadows.

This was no new emergency to the foreman, who ran for his snake-serum kit. Within minutes he had injected the serum and sent for a truck. He must get the boy to the nearby hospital as quickly as possible. It was there that I, the missionary nurse in charge, became acquainted with Salani.

"They won't listen to me," the foreman complained to the doctor. "Our strictest rule is that you never step off the path when you are picking leaves. But this boy is new, and his mind was on the leaves at the top of the bush."

"I wish someone had seen the snake so we would know the poison we're fighting," the doctor said. He looked worried. "The boy is already unconscious, so he must have gotten a large dose of it. We'll do the best we can, but you'd better send for the family."

"We don't know who they are nor where they live," the foreman said. "The boy came looking for work alone. He said his father was dead and the family had gone off, leaving him to look after himself. He's a good boy and a fast picker. Do your best for him, doctor." The busy foreman went back to his duties, thankful he could leave the boy in our hands.

I took over for the next 24 hours, and an African nurse and I did not leave him. We gave stimulants for the laboring heart and piled on blankets to warm the cold body. The boy looked shrunken and helpless as he lay unconscious in the hospital bed. But at the end of 24 hours we knew he would live. Prayer and modern medicine had won.

In the days that followed we were not able to win Salani's friendship. He lay silent and unsmiling, though the pain in his leg had lessened and he knew he would live. At first I thought that my foreign looks and less-than-fluent language frightened him. But the African nurse could not get a response out of him either. Even Muzampse failed. She was the ward housekeeper, and she had a way with frightened patients. Salani lay unmoving, his face a mask of unfriendliness and wariness.

I decided to try a solution I had used before. Down the hill from us was the mission school, and Temba was a student there. I sent word for him to come up after school.

"Temba," I said when he came, "thank you for coming so promptly. What would I do without you? We need your help with a snakebite case. The boy's name is Salani, and he's from the tea estate. He has no home, and he doesn't know where his family is. Please make friends with him. We've failed."

The first day Temba didn't get anywhere with the sick boy. But he had a remedy for that. The next day he brought his bush baby. That's what the Africans call the marmot. It's a small furry animal with little friendly eyes. African boys like to carry a marmot about in their pockets.

"I've brought my bush baby to stay with you while you're in the hospital," Temba said, handing Salani the little animal.

Salani took the gentle bush baby in his hands and spoke for the first time. "I had one once, but it died." Here was something he understood, something he could love. And that is how the boys became friends. But Salani still didn't like the rest of us.

"Can you read?" Temba asked Salani one day.

"I was just beginning to learn at the tea estate night school when this happened," he said.

"Would you like to study while you're here? I'll help you."

"Yes," the boy said. "I want to learn to read and write more than anything else."

"Tomorrow I'll bring up some books, and we'll see how far you've gone. I'll bring a tablet and pencil, too. You'll have plenty of time to study here, and you can keep up with your night school class," Temba said as he left.

That's the kind of boy Temba was. He belonged to the church youth volunteers, and this was the kind of service he liked most to give.

But Salani was puzzled. He asked, "Why do you come to see me? Is somebody paying you to teach me? What would you be doing if you weren't coming here?"

"Well," Temba said, rubbing the soft fur of the bush baby that sat beside Salani's pillow, "I come to see you because I want to. I hope we're going to be friends. Nobody pays me to teach you, and if I weren't here, I'd be playing soccer at school."

The next day I asked the African nurse to bundle Salani up and carry him out to the veranda for morning prayers. I sat by the railing looking down the hill to the narrow green valley with its small stream flowing through it. Across the valley a hill rose, not too steeply. It was dotted with the kraals and small farms of our African neighbors. I turned from this peaceful scene to look at Salani. He was sitting on the floor, his back against the wall, paying no attention to the service. Instead, he was looking down at the bush baby in his lap. As he rubbed its soft fur, an expression of contentment took the place of his usual scowl.

Day by day Salani improved. He lived for the afternoons and Temba's visits. One day he asked, "Why is everybody so good to me here?"

"Well," Temba said, "it's because they are Christians."

"What's *Christians?*"

"People who try to live like Christ."

"Who's Christ?"

"Let me read to you from my Bible to help you understand." Temba took his New Testament from his pocket.

"What's a Bible?" Salani asked.

"It's a book of history about Christianity and the life of Jesus. It tells us how to live good, useful lives."

Salani was puzzled.

"I'll tell you what," Temba said. "I'll ask our pastor to come and see you and to explain it all to you."

"What's a pastor?" Salani asked.

"He's the head person in our church," Temba said, using the only word he could think of that Salani would understand.

When the pastor came, the ward was in confusion. An accident case had come in, and I was helping the doctor. I suggested, "Why don't you carry Salani outside where it's quiet." The bush baby went along.

I heard the murmur of voices and knew that our good pastor was telling Salani about the heavenly Father and His Son. Going out to the kitchen for a kettle of hot water, I heard the pastor say, "There is great happiness in living the Christian life—"

Salani interrupted him. "Temba's a Christian, isn't he?" he said.

"Yes, he is, but what made you think so?" the pastor asked.

"Nobody but a Christian would bring his bush baby to keep me company."

At last Salani was well, and the time came for him to return to the tea estate. Temba came to the hospital to say goodbye. "We're friends now, aren't we?" I heard him say.

"Yes, we're friends." Salani took the bush baby out of his pocket and held it out to Temba. "Here's your bush baby. He helped the hospital people make me well."

"I want you to have him," Temba said. "He's

happy with you. Take him back to the tea estate with you."

Salani couldn't find the words he wanted to thank Temba. He could only look his thanks. He rubbed the soft fur gently and then put the bush baby back in his pocket.

"Come back in a week and go to church with me," Temba invited.

"I will if I can get permission," Salani said. "And I'll bring along the bush baby, because I'll never leave him alone."

"I know you won't," Temba said.

We watched thankfully as Salani turned and started his journey back to the tea estate six miles away.

"Walk well," Temba called.

8

The Power of a Girl

by Dorothy Aitken

just can't understand what's gotten into Kitty," Mike said to Dr. David when the owner came out to look at the horses one evening. "She's always seemed to be very fond of me, and we've always had fun working with the horses together."

"Why? What's happened?" Dr. David leaned on the corral gate and looked earnestly at this young man he had hired to care for his horses. "Kitty is the one who insisted that I hire you."

"I know." Mike took out a cigarette and lit it. After a few puffs he went on. "Lately she comes for a while, and we curry the horses and she braids their manes and tails. Then suddenly, just like that"— Mike snapped his fingers—"she begins to cry and runs into the house. I can't figure out what I do that makes her act that way."

"I'll look into it," promised Dr. David as he started toward the house. "If I can find out, I'll let you know."

Several days later as his daughter sat doing her homework after supper, Dr. David asked her about her strange behavior. "What makes you act that way around Mike?"

"What do you mean, Father?" Kitty looked up from her history book.

"He says that you work along with him for a while, and then suddenly you begin to cry and run into the house. You've got Mike mighty worried, Kit."

Kitty lowered her head. "I don't want Mike to die," she whispered.

"Well, what makes you think he's going to do that?" Dr. David asked.

Kitty remained silent for a long time.

"Come now, Kitty. Tell me. Mike wants to know."

"Mike smokes." Kitty stated the fact almost angrily. "And if he smokes, he's going to die of lung cancer." Kitty's eyes were brimming when she turned her face to her father. "You saw those awful pictures about lung cancer."

"Well, yes."

"And Mike smokes a lot. And you know, Father, that he's the best person with horses. That's why we hired him. He's so kind and gentle. He talks to the horses and treats them as if they were human. We could never find anyone like Mike to take his place."

"Well, he's not going to die right away," Father said. "But why do you suddenly start your crying right in front of him? Can't you wait till you get into the privacy of your own room?"

"I know, Father, but it happens every day. First we clean the stalls; then we give the horses their oats and curry them. And when that's done, there's a little break, and the first thing Mike does every day is take out a cigarette. I can just see him lying there in his coffin, white and cold."

"Now, look, Kit. There's nothing that will do Mike more good than for you to tell him yourself why you cry and run off every afternoon. Come, let's go out to Mike's room."

Kitty wasn't sure she wanted to go, but there wasn't much she could do about it, for Father was propelling her along with him.

"Mike, I've solved your puzzle," Dr. David announced when Mike opened the door.

Mike looked a bit surprised at his visitors and frantically began to pick up odds and ends lying around the room.

"Kitty is going to tell you about it herself," announced Father as Kitty hung her head.

"All right, why do you cry every afternoon when we're finished with the horses?" Mike sat down beside Kitty and nervously reached for a cigarette.

"Don't do that!" Kitty began to cry. Big, bellowing sobs went into the pillows on the sofa as she tried to bury her head. "You're going to die, Mike. You're going to die!"

"Whatever is she talking about?" Mike looked at Father with puzzled eyes.

"We saw a film a few weeks ago," Father explained. "It was about lung cancer, and she can't forget it!"

"Well?" Mike wasn't getting the point at all.

"Kitty heard the commentator say that every year 20,000 cigarette smokers die of lung cancer. Don't you see? Kitty is afraid that you are going to get lung cancer and die. Then who would take care of the horses?"

"H'mmm. Never thought of that." Mike put out his cigarette and bent over Kitty. "Look, Kit, if I promise to see that film, will you stop crying?"

Kitty nodded. "And will you promise not to smoke anymore?"

"I'll try," Mike said. *At least I won't smoke in her presence*, he thought.

He went to see the film and came home convinced. Kitty never saw him smoke again. Then Mike began to inquire into Kitty's faith. Why did she go to church on Saturday? Why did all the horses have to be groomed and finished before sunset on Friday night? There were many whys that Mike had to find out about. Kitty told him all that she knew.

One day Mike received a letter from the president, and like so many other men, he had to join the war in Vietnam. Kitty and her parents saw him off. "Be sure to keep the Sabbath," cried Kitty when the bus was about to pull out. "And never smoke anymore!"

Mike's duty in Vietnam was tough. How many times he escaped death he never knew, but the times he did know about were terrifying. Finally it came his turn for rest and recuperation, and he chose to go to Bangkok.

As soon as he landed in Bangkok, he asked about the Adventist hospital. Somehow he had never felt right all this time. No one seemed to care whether he lived or died, and he remembered Kitty often and her concern for his health. Maybe some other Adventists would be as interested.

Mike was welcomed with open arms into the Adventist community in Bangkok. They fed him. They prayed with him. The pastor studied with him, and before Mike returned home he was baptized.

And all that started with a little girl who cared.

9

Just Like Frank

by Doris B. Colligan

During all of Ray Brown's 14 years, he had heard the same question: "Why can't you be more like Frank?"

Ray adored his 22-year-old brother, who had recently gone into the Army. But try as he would, he could never come up to Frank's reputation.

Ray was all thumbs and kept bumping into things. When he tried to fix something, it turned out worse than when he'd started. "Oh, if you were only more like Frank," his exasperated parents would say.

Ray wasn't outstanding in school. He always passed, but with no brilliant marks. He was a plugger, while things had always come easily to Frank. When he didn't understand some of his schoolwork, teachers who had taught Frank a few years earlier would say, "Why can't you be more like your brother, Frank?"

But with all his faults, Ray kept trying. Sometimes

he would run errands or do favors for the neighbors. They were always polite to him, but Ray imagined they were saying, "Why aren't you more like your brother?"

Sometimes Ray thought even Frank's dog, Rex, didn't think he was much good. He would never mind Ray and would answer his call when he was good and ready. Even Rex was probably thinking, *Why can't you be more like my master? There was a guy!*

Ray had taken over the paper route that Frank had once had. He was sometimes slow in his deliveries, but he made up for this by being extra careful to put the papers where the wind or playful puppies couldn't destroy them. All his accounts were good except for Mrs. Marshall. He used to put in the money for her and sometimes made several trips to her home before she had the proper change.

He became well acquainted both with Mrs. Marshall and her little 3-year-old Jimmy. Mrs. Marshall, a newcomer to town and 300 miles away from her former home, was happy to talk to Ray. Her husband was overseas, with three more months in the military service before he could return. Also, Mrs. Marshall was one of the few people who hadn't known Frank, so she never compared Ray to his older brother.

One day Ray found Mrs. Marshall upset. She told him she needed to go to the hospital right away, for her second baby was due. Her mother couldn't arrive in town for several hours yet. "What shall I do about Jimmy?" Mrs. Marshall worried.

"Don't you mind about Jimmy, Mrs. Marshall," Ray said. "I'll take him home with me until your mother comes. You just go ahead and call a taxi. I'll wait here until it arrives."

Jimmy, who was fond of Ray, was excited at the prospect of going home with him. So he didn't even make a fuss when his mother went away in the taxi. He was just in a hurry to get to Ray's house and have Ray play with him.

Ray's surprised mother was very understanding about the little guest Ray had brought home. She acted as if it were the most usual thing in the world for him to take care of a 3-year-old. She made a quick decision. "I don't believe Mrs. Marshall should be alone at the hospital. If I stay with her until her mother arrives, do you think you could get supper for Dad and Jimmy?"

Ray was very sure he could. He decided to make pancakes and fried eggs and have some ice cream for dessert.

Both his dad and little Jimmy praised the supper. "M-m-m, good!" Jimmy said with appreciation.

"A chef from the Waldorf couldn't have done better," Mr. Brown added.

Ray smiled proudly, recalling he hadn't spilled or dropped a single thing. *I guess I was so busy that I forgot to think what Frank might have done*, he thought to himself.

Jimmy helped Ray clear the table, and they all did the dishes together. Ray kept Jimmy playing cars until Mrs. Brown came home.

A lovely older edition of Mrs. Marshall came home with Ray's mother. She was Mrs. Marshall's mother, Mrs. Graves.

"So this is the young man who has been so helpful to my daughter," Mrs. Graves beamed. "My daughter wanted me to tell you she has a beautiful little sister for Jimmy. I'll take him off your hands now. I don't know what we would have done without you."

Ray was really pleased with the unaccustomed praise. Maybe, he thought, *I can find other things to do so folks won't keep comparing me to Frank.*

He decided he would begin right away by taking some of the profits from his newspaper route to send some flowers to Mrs. Marshall. He picked out a pretty dish garden to send her at the hospital.

When Mrs. Brown learned about this, she said, "Why, son, what a thoughtful thing to do."

"I kept thinking about her husband so far away and her being a stranger," Ray said. "I thought she wouldn't be getting many flowers."

"You seem so grown-up all of a sudden," Ray's mother said, giving him a big hug.

"I'm trying to be just like Frank," Ray admitted.

"Just keep on being like Ray," his mother replied with a smile.

10

The Giving Christmas

by Nina Walter

Carolyn wanted just one thing for Christmas—a bright-red woolly sweater to wear to school. Her last year's sweater was worn and faded and had mended places that showed. Besides, it was too small for her. She didn't like to walk beside her best friend, Marian, who had a new blue sweater and a cap to match.

Carolyn had wished and hinted and asked and even prayed for a new sweater. But now she just tried not to think about it. For her father was without a job after the mill had closed.

"They all say to come back after Christmas," he reported one morning after a week of job searching. "I hope we can make the money last."

"We'll have to," Carolyn's mother said. "And we'll have to postpone our own Christmas plans."

She looked at Carolyn, and Carolyn knew she

ought to answer that look. She ought to say, "That will be all right." But she couldn't. She just hurried out of the house to join Marian, who was waiting at the gate to walk to school with her.

It'll be a terrible Christmas, she thought. For the first time in her life there wouldn't be a single Christmas gift for her. What would she say when the other girls showed her their gifts?

At school Carolyn and Marian joined the other students, who were waiting for the last bell to ring. They were talking about what they hoped to get for Christmas—bicycles, sleds, radios, new clothes. Those whose fathers, like Carolyn's, had lost their jobs when the mill closed weren't saying much, and Carolyn noticed that some of them looked as disappointed as she felt.

When their teacher, Miss Dodson, called the class to order she said a surprising thing. "I couldn't help overhearing your plans for *getting.* Why don't you try a *giving* Christmas for a change?"

"We do give," Marian said. "We always exchange gifts."

"I don't mean exchanging gifts with your family and friends," Miss Dodson explained. "I mean doing something for somebody who needs it, something that will be a surprise, a gift that you give without expecting to get anything back."

Everybody in the class liked the idea. They made

a list of the people they were going to surprise. Some decided to make or repair toys for small children. Some planned gifts or services for elderly people who lived alone. All of them would make their own Christmas cards to go with the gifts and list the services they intended to perform, such as sweeping sidewalks, stacking wood, or running vacuum cleaners. Miss Dodson let them use their art period for the Christmas cards. Carolyn and Marian worked on their cards together.

"I chose Susan Thompson," Marian said. "You know, the 5-year-old girl who broke her arm."

"What are you going to do for Susan?" Carolyn asked.

"I'm going to make some clothes for her doll and help her dress it," Marian replied. "What are you going to do?"

"I chose Mrs. Gleason, the old lady who lives next door to me," Carolyn said. "But I don't know what to do for her."

"You could give her one of your books," Marian suggested.

"She doesn't read much," Carolyn answered. "She just sits in her wheelchair and listens to her radio and crochets or knits."

All the way home Carolyn kept trying to think of something to do for her elderly neighbor. Mrs. Gleason was sitting in front of her window, as usual;

and as usual, her knitting needles were flying. When she looked up and saw Carolyn, she waved, and Carolyn waved back. And right then an idea popped into Carolyn's head.

She thought about the pile of old magazines in the attic. When she was younger she had enjoyed cutting pictures out of them. She remembered the needle-work pages and the scrapbook she had never used.

"Now I know what my gift will be," she said aloud as she hurried home to begin.

Every day for a week Carolyn spent some time in the attic, cutting and pasting. At last she had a scrapbook full of knitting and crochet patterns.

"I hope she likes it," she said as she showed her mother the book.

"I'm sure she will," her mother assured her. "She's always borrowing patterns from other people. You found some lovely ones in those old magazines."

On Christmas Eve, Carolyn wrapped her gift in some bright paper she had saved from the last Christmas. She tied it with a cord she had made by twisting red and green yarn together, and she slipped her Christmas card under the cord. Then she took the package to Mrs. Gleason.

"A present for me!" the woman exclaimed. "How lovely. I haven't had a present for ages. I wonder what it can be."

"Open it," Carolyn urged. "I made it myself."

When Mrs. Gleason saw what was in the package, she said, "Oh, my! You've given me a wonderful gift. I can't thank you enough. If only there was something I could do for you!"

"Oh, no," Carolyn said. "Our class made this a giving Christmas instead of a getting Christmas."

"That's a good idea," Mrs. Gleason said. "A giving Christmas. I'd like to have a part in it." She looked at Carolyn. "You need a new sweater; that one is about worn out."

"I know," Carolyn murmured.

"I have a lot of red yarn left over from the brother-and-sister suits I knitted for Mrs. Blake's twins," Mrs. Gleason continued. "How would you like to use it to make a sweater for yourself?"

"I couldn't," Carolyn said. "I don't know how."

Mrs. Gleason smiled. "If you come over after Christmas," she said, "I'll teach you to knit. Then you can make your own sweater. Would you like that?"

"Oh, yes!" Carolyn exclaimed. "I'd love to learn how to knit. Will you really teach me?"

"I'd love to," Mrs. Gleason said. "It will be fun."

And so Carolyn got a new sweater after all, and she had the fun of making it herself. And for a surprise, Mrs. Gleason made her a red cap to go with it.

11

"I Need You, Jeff"

by Marilyn Jensen

He arrived at the last minute, hoping the others would already be on the court practicing. But no such luck. As soon as he walked into the locker room, the boy next to him said, "Going to the Lakers game with us, Collins?"

Jeff shook his head, fighting to hide his disappointment. Let them think he didn't care. He didn't want to have to explain about Dad being laid off from work. The last thing Jeff wanted was someone feeling sorry for him. But it wasn't fair, he thought as he yanked open his locker. The others were always going someplace fun. Most of them didn't even think it was a big deal. Man, what he wouldn't give to see a live pro basketball game.

If only he could find a job. But there weren't many for boys his age in a small town such as

Chelsea. He had thought he had one a while back.

"Old Mr. Henderson's looking for a boy to help out in his grocery store," their minister had told Jeff one day. "Needs someone to stock the shelves and keep the place clean."

Jeff had hopped on his bike and gone right over.

"You look like you'd be a good worker," the old man told him, then shook his head. "But I'd really like someone a little older."

The same old story, thought Jeff.

The real blow was not so much losing the job but learning that Larry Phillips had gotten it. "He's only a year older than I am," Jeff said to his mother as he was eating supper that night. "And everyone knows he's the biggest goof-off in school." He pushed himself away from the kitchen table. "What does he need the money for anyway? His dad's loaded."

"Looks to me like you're suffering from a good case of envy-itis," Mother answered. "Here, maybe this will help." She handed him a cookie fresh from the oven. "Besides, just because his family has more money than we do doesn't mean Larry hasn't a right to work if he wants to. It will probably be good for him."

Jeff finished his cookie and reached for another.

"You've also got a touch of self-pity," Mother said, "which doesn't do you a bit of good." She smiled. "Think on the bright side. If you had gotten the job, how could you play on the basketball team?"

Jeff hadn't thought of that. She was right. If he had to work every day after school, he'd have to drop basketball.

"And there are worse things than missing the Lakers game," his mother said. "You can watch it on TV, you know. I'll even make popcorn."

Jeff grinned sheepishly. Mother always could make things seem better.

He had a few bad moments the day after the Lakers game, when he heard the others talking about it, but his mind was on the school basketball game the following Wednesday night. Chelsea High and St. Michaels were tied for first place. This was the game that would decide the championship, with the winners going to Centerville for the district playoff in a couple of weeks. Jeff spent every spare minute in his backyard practicing shots. He knew his weak point was passing, so he got the little neighbor boy to practice with him.

Receive, dribble, shoot . . . receive, dribble, shoot . . . It tired him out, but it was worth it. He could see the difference at practice.

"The way you're going, we're bound to win, Collins," the coach said to him as they went off the court the day before the game. "With you in there I have no doubt which way the game will go."

Jeff grinned. It was going to be some game.

The telephone woke him up Wednesday morning. *Who could it be at this hour?* he wondered as he staggered out of bed to answer it.

"Hello, is this Jeffrey Collins?"

"Yes." Jeff had heard that thin, reedy voice somewhere before, but where?

"This is Mr. Henderson. You know, the grocery store. Jeff, I'm sorry to call so early, but I'm in a spot. I'm not feeling too well, and I need someone to come in and help out in the store after school until 9:00 today and tomorrow. Do you think you'd be able to do it?"

Until 9:00 tonight? The night of the game? "But I thought you had Larry Phillips working for you," Jeff stammered.

"He was. Good worker, too, while he was here. But three days ago he asked for the rest of the week off. I told him I needed him, that I just can't get around that good anymore, but he said no, that he had something he had to do this week, that he'd be back next week." The old man paused. "I thought I could manage by myself, but I just can't. I really need you, Jeff. Can you come?"

Jeff gripped the receiver so tightly that his knuckles whitened. If only he could have heard those words three months ago. Or even before the Lakers game. Right now money meant nothing compared to that championship game. Jeff knew he had to say something.

"I'm . . . I'm sorry," he started to say, but his words were drowned out by a violent coughing seizure from the other end. It lasted so long that Jeff got worried. In his mind he could picture the frail little man and the disarray that was probably around him as he tried to help customers, along with everything else he had to do.

It was a full minute before Mr. Henderson could speak. "I'm sorry, son; I didn't hear you. What was that you said?"

"I said, of course I'll come," said Jeff.

After all, he wasn't the only player on the team. Both Ron and Bill were good too, and he knew that either of them would give their eyeteeth for the chance to play in the big game.

The hardest part was going to be telling the coach. Jeff's fingers shook as he dialed the number.

The way Mr. Henderson's pale eyes lit up when Jeff reported for work that afternoon took Jeff's mind off the game, and when he went to work sorting, re-filling shelves, and doing all the things that needed to be done, he was amazed at how fast the time went. It was time to close up before he knew it.

The coach himself called later that night to tell Jeff they had won. "We're counting on you for that playoff game in Centerville," he said. "Tonight's game was nothing compared to what we face there. See you at practice next week."

Jeff was still in a jubilant mood over the good news when he reported for work the next afternoon.

"I don't know what I did without you, Jeff," said Mr. Henderson when they got ready to close up that night. "You work rings around any boy I've ever seen." He hesitated, then said, "The job's yours regular if you want it. You start work Monday and work every day during the week except—" and his mouth twitched in a suppressed grin, "except next Thursday."

"Next Thursday?"

"Yes, I understand you can't work for anyone that day except for your school's basketball team at that district playoff game in Centerville."

"You know about that?"

Mr. Henderson nodded. "I've known your coach for years. He called me this morning. Just happened to mention what you gave up to help me yesterday." He put his arm around Jeff's shoulder. "You're quite a boy. You know, I've been thinking. It's a long time since I've seen the Lakers play. Maybe you and I could go to a game one of these days. As soon as I feel a little better I'll see about getting us a couple of tickets. How's that sound?"

Jeff was never sure afterward, but he thinks he floated instead of rode home on his bike. At least that's the way it felt.

12

A Sled for Catherine

by Nina Walter

Catherine didn't have a sled. She always had to wait for an invitation to ride with someone else down Slocum Hill. She often rode with her best friend, Emily, and sometimes Emily even let her steer. The other children offered her rides too—all except Clem, the new boy. Clem just taunted her about not having a sled. Clem had the best sled on the hill, a green racer, but he never offered a ride to anyone.

Waiting for Emily, Catherine gave the powdery snow a kick and almost lost her boot. It was a good, stout boot, but a size too large. Her boots, the coat with the sheepskin collar, and the cap with the sheepskin lining had belonged to her big brother Joey. At first, Catherine had felt uncomfortable wearing a boy's coat and boots and cap to the hill, but nobody had noticed or laughed. They seemed to know that you had to get along without new clothes and a sled when your father had a broken leg and could not drive his truck.

Then Clem had come to the hill with his fine new sled and had started making fun of her. He was the first to see her today.

"There's that girl who wears boys' clothes," he shouted. "Think you're tough? How about a fight, boy?" He doubled his fists and pranced in front of her.

Catherine stood still. "Even boys don't fight without a reason," she said. "Only bullies do."

Clem reached an arm straight out and gave her a shove, and Catherine fell backward into the snow. Then Clem jumped on his green racer and went flying down the hill.

Johnny pulled his sled to the top of the hill, hurried the last few steps, and reached out a hand to help Catherine up. "I saw what he did," he said. "Are you hurt?"

"No," Catherine answered, trying not to cry. She brushed the snow off her clothes and pulled Joey's cap down over her short brown hair. "He makes me so mad!"

"Forget it," Johnny advised. "Come on and ride with me down the hill."

Johnny's sled was homemade. It was heavy and slow, but it was larger than the others, and there was plenty of room for two or three to ride. Catherine liked to ride with Johnny. But on their first trip down the hill Clem tried one of his favorite tricks. He swerved his sled so close that he seemed about to hit them.

"Look out!" Catherine shouted.

But Johnny steered a straight course and did not even look at Clem. "If he runs into us," he said, "he'll get the worst of it. This sled's built like a truck."

"I wish he wouldn't do that," said Catherine. "Every time he comes at Emily and me like that, Emily swerves and we fall off, and then he laughs."

"It's dangerous," Johnny said. "He might hurt somebody."

Catherine sighed. "I guess he's trying to drive us off the hill, the way he drove the Merritt twins off the hill. They won't ride when he's around—and he's always around."

After the second ride Catherine thanked Johnny and sat down to wait for Emily. As she watched from the top of the hill, she saw Clem make another run at Johnny and then swerve away at the last second. His sled skidded out of control, slid across the side of the hill, and hit a big maple tree. Clem rolled to the bottom of the hill, and his sled landed on top of him. Emily arrived just as Catherine stood up to see better.

"What's the matter?" Emily asked. "What's going on?"

"It's Clem!" Catherine exclaimed. "He was pretending to ram Johnny, and he rammed the tree instead."

"And broke his sled, and maybe his head, I hope," Emily replied with a giggle. "Come on. Let's go see."

The two girls sailed down the hill on Emily's sled. Johnny was waiting for them.

"Well, Mr. Smarty-pants finally took a fall," he said.

"Aren't you going to see if he's hurt?" Catherine asked.

"If he needs help, he can ask," Johnny replied. "Then I'll go. But if I go now and he doesn't need help, he'll just insult me. He might even say I ran into him."

"But we saw what happened," Catherine said. "And he might really need help."

Clem sat up then and brushed the snow off his face. He turned his sled over and looked at it.

"I guess he's all right," Emily said. "Let's go back up the hill."

One by one the other children sledded down the hill and started back up. Nobody stopped to speak to Clem or to offer help. Catherine kept looking back.

"Something must be wrong with him," she said. "He's still just sitting there."

"He can yell if he needs help," said Johnny, who was walking beside the two girls.

Finally Catherine stopped. "I'm going back to see."

"After the way he treats you?" Emily yelled.

"You're crazy. Leave him alone. Maybe it'll teach him a lesson."

"I think he has already had a lesson," Catherine replied.

The hill was steep, and Catherine slipped and slid part of the way, but she finally reached Clem. He was sitting in the snow, and his face was streaked with tears.

"Get outta here!" Clem said angrily. "Leave me alone!"

"Is your sled broken?" Catherine asked.

"No, but I think my ankle is."

Catherine looked. Clem's right foot seemed to be twisted, and she could see that it was swelling above his shoe top. "Why didn't you call somebody?" she asked.

"Who'd have come?"

"Johnny would have come," she said. "If you can get on the sled, I'll pull you," she offered. "It isn't very far to your house."

Clem crawled onto the sled and stretched his injured foot out in front of him. Then Catherine started pulling the sled slowly along in the snow beside the sidewalk.

"I was mean to you," said Clem. "Why are you helping me?"

"Because you need help," Catherine answered, "and because I try to do the things Jesus wants me to do."

As they turned the corner at the end of the block, Clem said, "There's my dad's car—that blue station wagon. He's home early."

Clem's father saw them and hurried to help. "What happened?" he asked.

"I slid into a tree and hurt my foot," Clem explained. "Catherine helped me back from the hill."

Clem's father knelt and looked at the foot. "It may be broken. I'll carry you to the house and call Dr. Jamison. You're lucky to have a friend like Catherine."

Catherine could see Clem's face getting red. "She's a better friend than I've been, Dad. Is it all right if she uses my sled till my foot's better?"

His father smiled. "Sure, it's fine." He lifted Clem in his arms. "Take the sled," he said to Catherine. "And thanks for helping Clem."

"You're welcome," Catherine replied. She looked at Clem. "Are you sure you want to lend me your sled?"

"I'm sure," Clem said. "We're friends now."

"I'll take good care of it," Catherine promised.

As Catherine walked back to the hill, pulling Clem's green racer, she thought, *I guess Clem wanted to be friendly all along and just didn't know how.*

13

The Never-to-Be-Forgotten Birthday

by Rosaleen Schmutz

The week before his birthday, Eric received a letter from his uncle Don. Enclosed were three $1 bills. He read the letter carefully.

Dear Eric,

This isn't all that I'm giving you for a birthday present. You are getting bigger now, and so I am giving you a challenge. Use the enclosed money to buy something, and I will match it in value. If you buy something foolish, so will I. If you buy something worthwhile, so will I. It's up to you. I'll see you soon.

Uncle Don

"Look at this letter," Eric said to his sister, Becky, who was two years younger. "How about going shopping with me on Friday when school lets out early? You can help me pick out my present."

"I think that would be fun. But it's three more

days until Friday. That's a long time to wait."

"Not that long," her brother said, "and besides, I have to do some thinking first. I have to decide what would be foolish or not foolish."

"I think that's going to be a hard thing to do."

"I know it will be. And what's more, maybe what I don't think is foolish Uncle Don will."

Eric thought about it all day, and after supper that evening he wrote down a list of possible things he could get for three dollars: a new model plane, a light for his bike, another Hot Wheels car, a baseball.

"Have you made up your mind yet?" Becky asked Eric on Thursday morning as they walked to school together.

"Not yet," he said. "We can shop around tomorrow before I really decide."

"Well," said Becky, "I'm glad it's not today, because I have a scratchy throat."

By the time school was over, Becky's throat was worse.

"Your voice sounds funny," Eric told her on the way home from school.

"You aren't going to go to school tomorrow," her mother said when she looked at Becky's throat, "and what's more, I think you'll be staying in bed."

"But what about my shopping trip?" Eric wanted to know. "She promised to go shopping with me."

"We'll just wait and see how she is by tomorrow

afternoon," Mother said calmly. "She may be a lot better by then."

But she wasn't. In fact, Becky's voice was even more hoarse the next morning, and she had a fever. Eric knew there was no way she could go with him, so that afternoon he set out for the shopping center on his own.

He had pretty well decided he was going to add another car to his Hot Wheels collection. *No one could say that was a foolish present*, he thought to himself. But while he hunted for the Hot Wheels location in the new big store that had just opened, he came across something he just knew he had to have.

It was a giant-sized poster of a gorilla holding a sign that read: "Nobody is going to push me around."

I know the exact spot for it, Eric said to himself. *Next to the chest of drawers on the wall near my bed. That's going to be my motto, and I'll see it every day.*

After he paid his money and the store clerk handed him the long cardboard poster tube and his sales slip, Eric hurried outside and started for home. He could picture what his classmates would say when they saw it. When he got to the corner near his home, he began to run. He could hardly wait to hang the poster.

As the screen door slammed when he stepped into the kitchen, his mother called from the living room. "Is that you, Eric? Come here quickly."

Eric set the cardboard tube on the kitchen table and went into the room where his mother was sitting next to the telephone.

"I'm waiting for a call from Dr. Walker," she said. "Becky is worse than she was earlier today."

Before Eric could say anything, the phone rang. It was the doctor, and while his mother talked to him, Eric walked to his sister's room.

Becky opened her big brown eyes as he came close to her bed. Her face was red, and her light hair hung limply about her cheeks and forehead.

"Becky, are you all right?" Eric touched her hand.

"Just hot and thirsty," she said, "and I want to get up. There's nothing to do or see. Can't I get up?"

"Not for a while, dear," Mother said as she came in from the hallway. "Dr. Walker thinks you should stay in bed until every bit of fever is gone."

When she heard that, Becky started to cry.

"I wanted to go to the pet show this weekend," she said. "My friend Maureen is going to enter her lizard, Sloopy. It would have been fun to see."

"See you later, Sis," Eric called from the doorway. He waved his hand.

Back in the kitchen, he picked up the cardboard tube and stepped out of the house. This time he closed the door quietly, and then he ran back to the store.

Once inside, he glanced around to find the clerk who had sold him the poster. "I haven't even had it out of the tube," he said, "but I've changed my mind about it. Here is the sales slip."

"People don't usually return posters," the clerk said. "I believe you will have to talk to the store manager."

She rang a little bell next to the cash register. A few moments later a well-dressed woman walked down the aisle.

"What seems to be the problem with the poster?" the manager asked.

"There's no problem with the poster at all," Eric explained. "I didn't even take it out of the tube. It's just that my sister is sick and has to stay in bed, and I'd like to get something for her instead."

"I am sure that will be all right," the manager said. "Do you have any idea of what you would like to get her?"

"Oh, yes," said Eric quickly. "She needs a pet to keep her company. I'd like to buy a goldfish and a little bowl to keep it in so that she can watch it swim around while she has to stay in bed."

"Would you like some colored pebbles for the bottom? You'd have enough money for that, the bowl, and two fish. I believe your sister would like it."

"I know she would," Eric agreed. "She loves all kinds of pets."

The store manager put the bowl and pebbles into one bag and the two fish into a small plastic box that was filled with water. Eric carried them home carefully.

"They're for you," he told his sister.

"Oh, thank you very much!" Becky said, and she smiled as she watched Eric fix the pebbles in the bowl and pour the goldfish and the water into it. The fish seemed delighted with their new glass home and swam over the colored pebbles.

Becky watched them a few minutes, then turned to her brother. "Oh, Eric, I can't take these. You must have used up all of your birthday money for them."

"Why not, Becky?" Eric insisted. "It was my money, and I could use it any way I wanted to. I wanted to make you happy. Besides, I'll have fun watching the fish too, you know."

When Uncle Don arrived a few days later and heard the story of the two fish, he patted Eric's shoulder. "Congratulations, nephew. I see you met the challenge I gave you, and the gift you chose was a very thoughtful one indeed. Now I'd like you to take me to the store where you bought it."

"It's close enough to walk to," Eric said. He felt good to know his uncle Don was proud of him.

The store manager saw them come in. "How did your sister like her two new pets?"

"Just fine."

"And now," said Uncle Don, "we're looking for some additions to Eric's Hot Wheels collection. They're for his birthday."

"And this is for your birthday too," said the store

manager after Eric had chosen the Hot Wheels he wanted. She handed Eric a long cardboard tube.

"This is one birthday I'll always remember," Eric said as he thanked his uncle and the store manager for their gifts.

At home when Eric opened the cardboard tube, he found a little note rolled up inside: "Sorry the gorilla poster you selected was sold, but this one has a special message too."

Eric hung it up in the exact spot where he had planned to put the gorilla poster. Then he stepped back and looked at it. Under the picture of a large, happy elephant eating a huge peanut were the words "Good deeds always bring giant-sized happiness to others."

"That's something else I'll always remember," said Eric, and then he went to Becky's room to show her his new Hot Wheels.

Talk-Show Witnessing

by Edna May Olsen

Dad," Bret said one morning at breakfast as he reached for another slice of toast, "there are so many confused people in the world."

"I think you're right," his father commented. "But what prompted you to say that just now?"

"I've been listening to the talk show," Bret answered, "and it's hard to believe that a lot of people have no idea why the world is in such a mess."

"What's the talk show?" Mike, his younger brother, chimed in. "Is it something on the radio?"

"Yes," Bret explained. "It's on every afternoon and evening. Sometimes there's a guest, and after the guest speaks for a while, people can call in and ask questions. At least once a week the show has what's called open line—that's when there's no guest speaker. People just call up and say what's on their minds."

"I listen to it sometimes," Mom joined in the conversation. "They discuss quite a variety of subjects, including politics and religion. And I agree with you, Bret—often I'm amazed at the people's lack of Bible knowledge. So many listeners wonder what's happening, but don't know where to find the answers."

"That's right," Bret added. "One woman called up the other night and talked about the increase of crime in the world and asked the host what was going to happen to us. All he could say was her guess was as good as his!"

"What an opportunity for witnessing," Dad said thoughtfully. "Doesn't anyone ever tell the listening audience the real reason for all the crime and misery in the world?"

"Not that I've heard," Mom answered. "It seems that no one knows. Everyone just hopes that things will eventually get better."

"Someone should tell them," Bret commented. "Hey, that gives me an idea!"

Mike asked his brother a lot of questions about talk shows on their way to school that morning. Bret explained that talk shows are broadcast in most major cities and are an effective means for ordinary citizens to make their voice heard.

A few nights later Bret was listening to the radio program. A worried caller quizzed the host as to what he believed was causing all the problems the world is now facing. The host said he felt that things weren't any worse than they had been years ago, but that because of television and radio people were hearing more about them. The woman wasn't satisfied and wondered where she could go for answers.

Bret opened the door to leave his room. Everyone else had gone to bed, so he crept silently down the stairs and into the family room. He dialed the phone number he knew by heart. After a long wait, he heard the voice of the talk show host on the other end of the line.

"Good evening," welcomed the host, "you're on the air."

Bret's heart almost stopped beating. Too nervous, he couldn't utter a sound.

"Line one, are you there? Say something," coaxed the host, "or I'll have to go to another line."

Bret gulped and took a deep breath. "I just wanted to tell the lady why things are so bad in the world," he said timidly.

"How old are you?" questioned the host.

"Twelve," quavered Bret.

"Well, young man, what do you think is wrong with the world?"

Bret found his courage strengthening. "The reason the world is so bad is because of sin. Things will never be any better until Jesus comes, and then there'll be a new heaven and a new earth."

"You don't say." The host was serious. "Where did you get this information?"

"It's all in the Bible," Bret continued, warming to the conversation.

"I'm delighted to have the privilege of listening to you," the host said, "and I find it amazing that a young fellow like you knows so much. I wish I could have your faith," he continued.

"Oh, you can," Bret said excitedly. "It's so simple. Just ask Jesus to help you. He's promised that He—"

"Phone again soon," the host cut in, "but right now I must go to another line."

A few evenings later Bret made his second call to the radio program. This time talking was easier. The host remembered him and said that he'd received many favorable comments on Bret's first call. "Take all the time you need tonight," he encouraged.

A few minutes later Bret ended the conversation by suggesting that the listeners obtain a copy of *The Great Controversy* from the local Seventh-day Adventist church where he was a member. "This book explains in more detail what I've just talked about—and it's free."

To Bret's surprise, the host agreed to stop by the Adventist church for one when he was in the vicinity.

The next morning Bret told his family about the two calls. Dad looked a little concerned when Bret mentioned he had invited the listeners to ask for free copies of *The Great Controversy*. "Do you realize how many people heard you last night? Could be as many as a hundred thousand! I'd better alert our pastor so he'll have a large supply on hand."

"But Dad," Bret exclaimed after his father got over the initial shock, "I was able to speak to all those people about Jesus! Don't you think it was worth it?"

"I certainly do," Dad answered. "We should witness whenever and wherever we can—all it takes is being willing to use our time for God. I'm glad to see you understand what Jesus means when He tells us to go into all the world and preach the gospel.* You reached a large audience last night!"

—————

* Mark 16:15

Dark Shadow
on the Tracks

by Jan S. Doward

The sudden rumbling, rattling sound jolted the little house on the hillside. Nora's head jerked up.

"What was that?" she asked as she quickly dried her hands and ran to the kitchen door.

"Oh, it's nothing but the railroad handcar going back to town with the work crew," her mother replied.

But Nora knew her mother's hearing wasn't all that sharp, and she shook her head slightly. "Well, I never heard it make a sound like that before. It sounded more like a coal car dumping a whole load on the tracks. I've got a good notion to go down to the tracks and see what it was."

"Oh, you're just trying to get out of doing the rest of the dishes," Mother countered. "Take a look at the clock. You can see it's just about time for the work crew. They'll barely make it to the station and lift their handcar off the tracks before the Rio Grande express goes by."

Nora didn't argue with her mother. She whisked through the rest of the dishes as fast as she could, slipped on her jacket, and headed down the steep path to the tracks below their house. Way off in the distance she could hear the evening express whistle as the sound echoed down the valley. It was twilight now, and she knew the passenger train was skirting the great bend several miles away, steadily making its way along the flanks of the Colorado Mountains.

Back in those days before there were any diesel engines, the trains were run by steam, and their whistles made that mournful sound that carried very far away. Often Nora used to hear its faint sound from their house perched several hundred yards above the tracks, and she would hurry down to stand by the tracks in the evening and wave at the passenger train as it zoomed past. The evening express was always special to her. The cars, all lit up, seemed cozy inside, and to Nora the passengers looked well-dressed and rich. She'd stand by the tracks in the twilight, waving and waving until she could see only the bobbing red-and-green signal lights of the observation car.

"I wonder where all those people come from and where they're going," she would often say to herself.

But this evening she wasn't interested in waving,

nor was she thinking about all those rich people riding to the big city. She just had to find out what had made that rumbling sound. The fact that the Rio Grande express was headed her way only made her scamper faster. Yet she didn't dare stumble and fall on the steep path right then. About halfway to the tracks, she stopped. Right there on the tracks below her she could see a huge dark shadow.

"What could that be?" she asked out loud. She sucked in her breath as she made out the shape of a huge boulder about as high as her waist. Scattered all around were lesser rocks. Somehow, when the handcar had gone by, it had jarred the rocks loose from the steep bank, and they had rolled right down on the tracks.

"So that's what we heard!" Nora exclaimed.

She looked up again when the faint whistle of the evening express sounded. It would be here in about five minutes. Putting her shoulder to the big rock, she tried pushing with all her might, but it didn't budge. She stooped down to lift the smaller ones, but even they were so heavy that she could move them only slightly. Desperate now, she tried pushing the big rock again.

"It's no use!" she cried. "And the train will be here soon!"

Leaving the tracks, she scrambled up the bank and ran as fast as she could up the path to her house.

Her lungs felt as though they would burst as she panted her way to the back porch.

"Quick, Mother, quick!" she shouted. "The oil can! The oil can!"

She stooped down and picked up a stick of dry pine by the path. Grabbing the kerosene can from the porch, she unscrewed the lid and dashed oil all over the end of the stick. She had seen her father do this once when he was in need of a quick light.

Nora's mother stood in the doorway, her eyes wide with bewilderment. "Are you crazy, child?"

But Nora brushed past her mother and stuck the end of the stick into the woodstove. Instantly, she had a torch. Holding her blazing light high above her head, she raced back down the path to the tracks. By now Nora could hear the pounding of the great steam engine as it thundered closer to the spot where the boulder lay across the track. She quickened her pace. "I've got to make it!" she panted.

She slid down the bank to the tracks, using one hand for balance and the other for holding the torch high. Running toward that train in the gathering darkness was scary. But Nora knew that if she didn't make it in time to stop the train, it would derail, plunge over the steep bank on the other side, and roll to the valley far below.

The brilliant headlight struck Nora full in the face when it rounded the curve. She desperately waved and waved her torch. The whistle blew so loudly that it seemed as if it would burst her eardrums and blast her right off the track. Now the train was almost on top of her, and still she stood her ground, waving and waving her blazing torch. She wondered if the train would ever stop. The whistle blew non-stop now with an earsplitting force that sent shivers up and down her spine.

Finally, at the last second, she leaped aside as the engine roared past. But just as it did, the great drive-shafts stopped and the brakes locked the wheels, sending sparks flying to either side. The whole train edged all the way around the next corner before finally stopping, with the cowcatcher nudging the big boulder on the track.

The engineer and his assistant leaped from the cab and hurried forward to see what was on the track. Nora came panting up with her torch. She wasn't waving it anymore. The passengers poured from the cars and crowded around.

"What's the matter? What's the matter?" they cried.

"Matter enough!" answered the engineer. "Take a look at that boulder on the track." He pointed to the rock and then back at Nora. "If this girl hadn't warned us, we'd have plunged to our deaths for sure."

Everyone seemed to be asking questions all at once, and Nora did her best to explain just what had happened and how she had hurried to warn the train. It wasn't long before one of the men took off his hat and passed it around. In a few minutes it was filled with money clear to the brim.

"But I didn't do it for pay," said Nora. "And besides, it wasn't much to do. It wasn't worth so much money. Honestly, I didn't do it for . . ."

But her words were lost in praise and appreciation from the passengers and crew alike.

The conductor patted Nora on the shoulder. "That was a brave act. You've saved many lives tonight. None of us will ever be able to repay all that we owe you."

That night when all was finally quiet, she lay in her bed, staring into darkness but wrapped in a blanket of deep happiness. She had more money than she had ever had in her life, but that wasn't why she was so happy. A joyful thought echoed in her mind, singing her to sleep. *I stopped the train! I stopped the train!*

16

Reunion at Collinsville Creek

by Alvin B. Lebar

The doctor sighed wearily. "Your boy's legs have got to be exercised for at least an hour a day if he's ever to walk again."

Mother slumped against the door. Where could she find the money for such treatments? For that matter, how would she get me, only 6 years old then, to the rehabilitation center, even if she had the money?

Our small Tennessee town had been hard-hit by the Depression. We had moved there after the bank auctioned off our Virginia home when Mother could no longer make the payments. The only place she could find for us to live was a tiny apartment over the town bar.

Then, as if money problems weren't enough, a polio epidemic swept through the community. Houses all over town wore the forbidding red quarantine sign by their front doors. And now there was one by ours.

When the doctor had gone, Mother left immediately for the small rural hospital across town.

"I'm sorry, Mrs. Bannon," the nurse told her. "Our rehab facilities are already overloaded. The few children we are accepting must be able to travel here for therapy. Perhaps you'd like to put your son's name on our waiting list."

Mother turned away then, tears blinding her eyes, and stumbled out the door.

An office clerk, who'd overheard the conversation, dashed into the street after her. "Wait, Mrs. Bannon! Please!" she panted, catching up.

"You heard what the nurse said." Mother lifted a tear-streaked face. "There's no help for my boy."

The clerk put an arm around Mother. "It's only an idea, but I think it will work. My nephew Matt is only 12, but he's old for his age and good with kids. I just know he could learn those exercises and come by your house several times a week to help your boy." She paused, looking anxiously into Mother's face. "Children do learn from each other, you know."

And that's how Matt Daley became my "physical therapist." As far as I could tell, his only credentials were that his aunt worked at the hospital. After the county nurse gave him a few basic instructions, he came by after school three times a week.

I was very young then, and my memories of that time are mostly shadowy recollections. But I remember Matt gently coaxing my legs to respond, whispering little made-up rhymes to ease the long, painful exercises. With infinite patience he'd stretch my stiffened muscles again and again, until I was nearly exhausted. Then he'd quickly catch me before I fell.

When we were through for the day, he'd carry me out to the kitchen and pour each of us a glass of milk. Before lifting the glass to his lips, Matt would always bow his head in silent prayer.

Eight months later Mother and I had to move once more. By this time, because of Matt's persistence, I was able to stand and could even manage one or two shaky steps. In time I would recover almost completely. In the years that followed, we rarely spoke of that desperate time. Maybe it was too painful to remember. Or maybe we were simply too busy trying to keep alive.

Many years went by, and on a visit to the South, I found myself less than 100 miles from that small town where I had taken my first faltering steps to regain the use of my legs. Suddenly I knew I had to find Matt Daley.

There wasn't much information to go on. All I really had was a name and our old address. The red-haired man at the counter of Purdy's General Store didn't know a Matt Daley, but suggested that I talk to an old-timer who lived a few doors down the block.

When I arrived, the old man was seated comfortably on his front porch, reading the newspaper. He cupped a hand behind one ear. "Matt who?" he yelled in response to my question.

"Daley," I repeated.

"Well, no, can't say I know the name. You say Daley? Now, wait a minute. There's a fella named Matt who still lives somewhere around here. Used to work at the mill." He scratched his chin as he thought. "Retired some months back. Said he was feelin' poorly. Don't know his last name, though. Hold on." He opened the screen door and shouted inside. "Aggie!"

"Yeah," a voice responded from within.

"What's Matt's last name?"

"Who?"

"Matt. You know, the fella who just retired from the mill. He came by here a while back. Lives down near the McCullen tract. Always wears a big old hat. Keeps pretty much to himself. What's his last name?"

"I dunno," Aggie yelled. "Ain't it Taylor or something?"

"Might it be Daley?"

"That's right. Yes, that's what it is. What do you want to know for?"

The old man pushed his paper aside and stood up. "There's a man here lookin' for him."

A large woman appeared at the door holding a towel. "Well, if it's the Matt I'm thinkin' of, you won't find him at home this time of day. Not with fishin' season open."

"Aggie's right," the man agreed. "He'll be fishin' down at Collinsville Creek. You drivin'?"

I nodded.

He pointed down the street. "Well, take this road as far as you can, and then bear right and go until you can't go no farther. That'll be the creek. You'll find him there."

The creek was actually a branch of the Roanoke River and was the size of a small lake. As I parked my car, I spotted a man pulling his skiff ashore. "You'll probably find Matt Daley at the edge of the creek near the twin oaks," this man told me. "If he's in his spot, you can't miss him."

I walked for what seemed like a mile along a narrow path, finally coming out in a clearing. A man wearing an overlarge, floppy rain hat sat on a flat rock at the creek's edge. His back was toward me as he worked over some fishing tackle. I watched him in silence for a few moments.

Then the bending figure straightened and turned around, looking at me quizzically. Slowly, he placed his rod on the ground and removed his hat, revealing wisps of thinning gray hair. I stared as he moved toward me. As he walked, he dragged a lame right foot.

For the first time, I realized that Matt Daley had been a polio victim himself. My mouth went dry. I groped for words, trying to connect pieces of the past, explaining who I was and why I was there.

He listened silently. Then nodding, he suddenly grasped my arm, pulling me forward. "Remember!" he laughed. "'Course I remember!"

I stooped and gathered up his fishing gear. Together we began the long walk back.

17

How I Grew Eight Feet in Sixth Grade

by Karl Haffner

Suddenly I felt two feet tall. Just as I was strutting past my secret heartthrob—Linda, the petite blond beauty queen of Cedar Brook School—Mike started his joshing.

"Hey, Karl," Mike chided, "I heard you signed up for a computer dating service and they sent you the number for Dial-a-Prayer!"

Linda and her clique erupted in giggles.

"You have the intelligence of a stop sign," I fired back. *Someday,* I determined as I raced to math class, *I'm going to show that bully Mike. Maybe then Linda will like me.*

"OK, class, let's get started," Mr. Taylor announced as we shuffled to our desks. "Today we're going to learn more about long division. You will remember that yesterday we talked about . . ."

Mr. Taylor's class was always my favorite—only because he was so into his arithmetic on the chalkboard that he never noticed me reading *Hockey* magazine.

As I scanned an article about the Montreal Canadiens, an ad caught my eye. An ad that would change my life—or so I thought.

"Tired of being a wimp?" the ad questioned. "Are you fed up with being pushed around? Sport the muscles of Mr. Atlas! Snag the woman of your dreams. This secret weapon to eternal health is guaranteed, or your money back! Send only $19.95 to: Muscles, P.O. Box 44462, Livingston, NJ 07039."

That'll show Mike, I daydreamed. *What will he think when Linda's chasing me?*

I envisioned Linda coddling my bulging biceps. "Oh, Karl," I imagined her saying, "do you mind if I call you Mr. Jock, or do you prefer Mr. Health?"

"Mr. Health," I mused. "It's got a nice ring to it. Maybe I'll host my own TV show someday—Mr. Health's Aerobic Hour."

At last the package arrived in the mail. I ripped into it like a kid at Christmas. It dropped to the floor. In shock, I stared.

Four long silver springs with red handles on both ends. That's all it was. *How can that cheap contraption make me Mr. Atlas?* I wondered. Yet to snag Linda and snuff Mike, anything seemed worth a try.

Every night I tugged and yanked and pulled and

sweated. Sweat seemed to be my body's way of crying. "No pain, no gain!" I grunted as I strained and stretched the handles. But regardless of the ferocious workouts, my body still looked about as brawny as an X-ray.

"Mom," I questioned one evening, "how can I get big muscles?"

"There's more to good health than big muscles," she answered. "You have to exercise, sleep right, drink water, eat spinach and broccoli and turnips, and . . ."

"OK, Mom, I get your point."

I tried different types of exercises. I pumped iron. (Since I didn't have any weights, I worked out with my mother's iron.) I slept more. I guzzled more water. I ate spinach. I ate broccoli. As for the turnips, I wasn't that desperate yet.

A month slipped by. Nobody accused me of taking steroids. Nobody called me Mr. Atlas. Nobody called me Mr. Health.

But with a little imagination, and with the right light and mirror, and if I flexed hard enough, I could detect the beginning hint of ripples that resembled biceps.

But Linda never noticed.

"Dear God," I prayed one evening, "I hate myself. In fact, everybody hates me. Mike has all the muscles and girls and friends, and I don't have anything. How can I get Linda to notice me?"

God didn't answer—until the next day at school.

"It's time for recess," Mr. Taylor announced.

I raced to the restroom to change into a new Gold's Gym tank top. I figured the day had come for me to flaunt my new physique.

Just as I was leaving the restroom for the ball field, I heard a whimper in the stall. Freezing in my tracks, I asked, "Who's in there?"

"Nobody," replied the whining, squeaky voice.

Pulling the stall door open, I stared at a chubby little boy slumped in the corner. His tears burned reddish trails down his pudgy cheeks. "What's wrong?" I asked.

"Oh, nothing."

"What's your name?"

"Oh, nothing."

"That's not your name."

"Hank."

"Hank, huh?" Even though sixth graders didn't usually bother to talk to first graders, it seemed that it'd be OK this time.

"Yeah, Hank's my name," he whimpered.

"What are you crying for?"

"'Cuz everybody hates me."

"Aw, come on now, Hank. Not everybody hates you," I replied as I handed him a wadded ball of toilet paper. "Here, let's dry those tears. I don't hate you. And God doesn't hate you."

"But everybody calls me Fatso," Hank sniffled.

"Yeah, I know how it feels. Everybody calls me

Shortcake. Think of it like this: our bodies can only get better, right? Tell you what—I'll start calling you Shortcake if you'll start calling me Fatso. It'll be our secret code. What d'ya say? Deal?"

A slight grin curved his lips. "Can we do that?"

"Sure, I don't see why not."

By the time I coaxed Hank back to his classroom, recess was half over. It seemed like a good excuse not to bother with modeling my new tank top. *There's not enough time for Linda to really savor my new and improved biceps,* I rationalized. Besides, after helping Hank, for some reason my muscles just didn't seem so important.

The next Monday morning the most unbelievable thing happened. It was more unimaginable than Santa Claus shaving. It was more unlikely than putting out a raging forest fire with saliva.

It was incredible: Linda talked to me! For the first time of the school year Linda talked to me!

"Hi, Karl," she greeted.

"Um, ah, uh, um, hi there, uh, Linda," I stuttered.

"Did you do your math assignment?"

"Yesterday. I mean, yes, yesterday, um, I mean, yes, I did it."

"It wasn't too hard, was it?"

"Yes, yester . . . no, I mean, not really yesterday, it wasn't . . . ." My face felt as if it could glow in the dark.

"Yeah. Say, Karl, I just wanted to say, um, that was nice. What you did last Friday."

"Last Friday?"

"Yeah, I mean with Hank."

"Hank? Oh, yeah, Shortcake."

"He gets picked on a lot. Ever since Friday you've been his hero."

"Really? Why is he, I mean, what did you, I, uh, how do you know who Hank is?"

"He's my cousin. We went over to Aunt Sharon's house for Sabbath dinner. Hank told me about—"

"Cousins!" I blurted out. "You and Hank are cousins! I didn't know that."

"Nobody in the school knows. Oh, there's the bell. It's time for class. But thanks, that was nice. See ya!"

Suddenly I felt 10 feet tall.

18

Skinny Michal and the Cave of Machpelah

by Ralph E. Hendrix

I felt a shiver in spite of my warm pajamas. Mother was sitting on the edge of my bed, asking if I would help Father explore a cave.

"A cave? One in the desert?" I asked. (I had heard a lot about caves in the wilderness, like those where the Dead Sea scrolls were found.)

"No, Michal [pronounced mi-KEL]." She paused for a second.

In confusion I sat up, the bedclothes swirling around me. I could tell this was going to be an important cave by the way Mother paused.

"Father says it's the Cave of Machpelah."

"Machpelah! That's where Abraham and Sarah were buried!" I fairly shouted. I had learned in school of how Abraham buried his wife, Sarah, in the cave he bought from Ephron the Hittite. Abraham, Sarah,

Isaac, Rebekah, Jacob, and Leah—all those famous men and women were buried there. And they were asking me, Michal, to explore the cave!

"They've tried grown-ups," Mother continued, "but they're all too big. Father thought you would be perfect."

She kissed me good night and turned off the lights.

I lay in the dark, imagining the cave. *Just think. Me! Skinny little me! The one the kids always tease and call names!* Finally I fell asleep.

Father woke me hours later. It was still dark. He leaned over me. "You're not scared, are you?" he asked. "Ghosts? Spirits?"

I shook my head no.

"Maybe they will come and whisk my skinny little girl away!" he teased and gave me a hug. But this teasing was different. We both knew that I didn't have to be embarrassed about my size anymore. Because I was skinny, I could do what no one else could: I could enter the Cave of Machpelah.

I giggled and said, "Father, you know there are no such things as ghosts. Show me one, and then maybe I'll be afraid!"

His face got serious. "No, my little Michal, there will be no ghosts. But it might be dangerous. No archaeologist has ever been in the cave, and no Jew has been inside in 700 years. We're not sure what's in-

side. You don't have to go in if you don't want to."
He looked into my eyes.

I looked back. "Father, I'm not a little girl anymore. I'm 12 years old. I can do it."

I quickly dressed, piled into the backseat of the car, and bundled up in a blanket. It was very cold. I paused a moment to remember the day: Wednesday, October 9, 1968. A day I would remember the rest of my life. The day I would enter the Cave of Machpelah.

It didn't take us long to reach Hebron. The car stopped at some old buildings, and I got out, still wrapped in the blanket because of the cool night air.

As I walked with Father into the mosque, I felt a little odd: me, a Jew (and a girl, at that), in an Arab mosque. But once I got inside, I could see that the place was filled with soldiers, both men and women, all moving about on what looked to be very important business. I wasn't the only one "out of place."

A young man approached Father, and I could tell from his looks that he was talking about me. But I was more interested in the beautiful red-and-white marble walls, gold writing, and huge arches over magnificent pillars.

"But you think you can do it?" I heard someone ask.

"Michal? Michal, answer the general."

I looked at the man before me. He was bent on

one knee and had a bald, shiny head and an eye patch tight across his forehead. It was General Moshe Dayan, Israel's minister of defense!

He spoke again. "You're a young one, all right. But you think you can do it?" General Dayan reminded me of my grandfather.

"Yes, sir, General! And I'm not afraid of ghosts or spirits!" I blurted.

The whole room erupted in laughter. I felt my cheeks flush. But he laughed right along with the rest and even put his arm around my shoulders as he led me over to the cave entrance.

The hubbub of soldiers had died off now. Everyone was watching us. General Dayan patted my shoulder. "We have a brave volunteer right here. Ready and willing. Not even a few scorpions or snakes would bother her! Isn't that right, Michal?" He turned to me.

I nodded yes, not sure whether he was joking or not. *Maybe there are snakes and scorpions*, I thought. By now we were standing by the hole. Those 11 inches looked pretty small.

Father stood beside me as General Dayan explained what I must do. Someone was tying a rope around me to lower me down. First, I was to go down with a flashlight and a candle. If the air was bad, then the candle would flicker out. But if the air was good, I was to take a camera and some paper, and take pictures and draw and measure, just like a real archaeologist.

I stepped into the hole. First my legs. No problem. Then my hips and waist. One arm and shoulder disappeared as I wiggled. I felt another shiver run up my spine, but this time it was because I was hanging midair in the darkness of a cave that no one had gone into for years. My shoulders were almost too wide, but if I twisted just so . . . There!

I was inside, swinging by the rope.

They handed me the flashlight and candle, and lowered me. I landed on a heap of papers and paper money—offerings to the saints. I looked at the candle flame, trying to detect even the smallest of flickers. Rock-steady. The air was good!

They gave me more rope, and I explored the square room I was in. On the opposite wall three tombstones flickered in my candlelight. I shined the flashlight on them. The middle, taller one was decorated with Arabic writing. I looked away from the tombstones and continued to explore the cave— through a small opening in a wall, down a narrow corridor to steps that led up to the ceiling. I retraced my steps, and they pulled me up.

I told them all I had seen, and then the real work began. In all, I entered the cave five times during that long night.

I measured and mapped out the cave. I photographed the rooms, the tombstones, the corridor, and the stairs. I made sketches, paced distances, noted details—all the time marveling that no one else had ever done this, not even the greatest scholar.

It's been years now since that cold October night, and I have thought about it many times. I remember how a skinny little 12-year-old was the only one who was able to do what needed to be done. I learned that even though I'm not the strongest or the fastest or the smartest person in the world, with God's help I can still be the best person I can be. And I've tried to live like that all these years since I, skinny Michal, entered the Cave of Machpelah.

19

Sally's Rescue

by Richard Edison

Sally! Sally! Where are you?" Ricky's worried voice echoed off the wooded hills behind his house. It was time to leave for church, and Ricky's dog, Sally, a collie–Saint Bernard mix, hadn't returned from her morning run. His pet usually came right away when he called her. But after 15 minutes with no sign of Sally, Ricky became concerned.

"Ricky, we have to go now!" His mother's tone warned him not to argue.

With a last glance at the woods, Ricky reluctantly climbed into the van.

"She'll be fine," his mother said as they drove away. "I'll bet she'll be waiting in the driveway, covered with burdocks, when we get home."

"But it's cold out," Ricky said. "What if she gets sick?"

"With that thick coat of fur? I don't think so!" Mother replied with a laugh.

Unconvinced, Ricky sank back in his seat with a worried look on his face.

At Sabbath school Ricky asked Mrs. Marvin, his teacher, to have special prayer for Sally.

"Dear Jesus," the woman prayed, "Ricky's dog, Sally, is missing, and he is very worried. We know that even the animals are under Your care. Please bring Sally safely home, if it is Your will. Thank You, Lord. Amen."

When she'd finished praying, Mrs. Marvin gave Ricky a hug and said, "Don't worry. God will take care of Sally." Somehow Ricky sensed she was right.

That morning three boys, Casey, Brian, and Troy, were walking by the river near Ricky's house. It had snowed the night before, and the friends were headed to the big hill outside of town for some tobogganing. With cold, crisp air and bright sun, it was going to be a great day.

Laughing and throwing snowballs, they came to the bridge that crossed the river. Suddenly Brian stopped in midstride and listened.

"Hey, guys, did you hear that?"

"Hear what?" Casey asked.

"A dog barking," Brian replied. "Sounds like it's in trouble."

Straining to hear, the boys leaned over the bridge railing. In the distance, way up the river, they could just hear the faint yelps of a dog that was in distress.

Crossing the bridge, they raced up the trail beside the river, their toboggans bumping behind them. Around a sharp bend, they spotted a dog frantically trying to climb out of a hole in the ice at the center of the river. They could see that the animal had been there for a while, as her efforts were growing weak. Her bark had become a feeble whimper.

"Quick, we've got to help her!" cried Troy as he started out onto the ice.

"Wait!" Brian shouted. "The ice is too thin! You'll fall in too!"

"But we can't just leave her there. We've got to try!" Troy pleaded.

"OK, but wait. I've got an idea. Lie down on the ice first. That'll spread your weight out. I'll grab your feet, and Casey will hold mine. Then you can slither out to the dog."

Troy slid onto the ice and crawled slowly toward the hole where the dog struggled. He could feel the ice cracking under him, but it seemed to be support-ing him. It was reassuring, though, to feel Brian's strong grip on his ankles.

Inch by agonizing inch the human chain snaked across the frozen river toward the dog. By now the animal had ceased struggling and was resting with her paws on the ice's edge. The dog's eyes had glazed over with exhaustion. She seemed not to notice the boys as they gradually worked their way toward her.

At last Troy arrived at the edge of the hole. "Easy, girl," he said quietly as he gently grabbed hold of the dog's paws. Then he called back to Brian and Casey, "I've got her! Pull!"

Suddenly the dog made a desperate lunge. Troy felt the ice shift and then crack beneath him. Freezing water filled his mouth. "Help!" the boy cried. Then he and the dog plunged into the water, his two companions unable to hold on.

Brian and Casey watched in horror as their friend disappeared into the dark water.

In shocked silence they stared at the shattered hole where they'd last seen Troy. Suddenly their buddy's head broke the water's surface, followed by the dog's!

Brian stayed on the ice while Casey hurriedly crawled back to shore to grab a toboggan. He slid it out to Brian before grabbing his ankle again. Brian held on to the rope as he eased the toboggan toward Troy. With one half-frozen hand Troy grabbed the sled. With the other he lifted the dog onto it and then yelled, "Pull!"

Casey had hooked a leg around a tree root on shore, and he and Brian began to pull with all their strength. Slowly, agonizingly, the toboggan, with its shivering, water-soaked cargo, began to move over the ice. After what seemed like hours, they reached the shore and fell exhausted in a heap together.

Stirring finally, Troy groaned, "I'm freezing! Let's

get home. We'll pull the dog on the toboggan; she's too weak to walk."

Slowly they dragged themselves toward Troy's house, the dog lying exhausted on the toboggan behind them.

Troy's mother gasped when the boys stumbled through the door. She sprang into action, wrapping them and the dog in warm blankets. As she made hot chocolate, she called a veterinarian on the phone. Soon the vet arrived, and he loaded the bundled-up dog into his truck. Driving away, he shouted back, "You boys are heroes!"

A ringing phone greeted Ricky and his parents when they arrived home. "I've got your dog!" Ricky heard the veterinarian exclaim when he picked up the receiver. The boy listened excitedly, then relayed the good news to his parents. As they rushed out to the car, Ricky looked up and whispered, "Thank You, Jesus, thank You!"

One month later Ricky stood proudly with Sally, now completely recovered from her frigid swim, in front of a TV camera at the local station. With them stood three camera-shy boys, Casey, Brian, and Troy, waiting to receive the Lassie award for their bravery. Sally barked her approval when the awards were handed out, making the audience laugh.

Later, after thanking the boys again, Ricky walked with Sally outside the TV station. Watching the sunset over the snow-covered hills, Ricky thanked God again for His love and for rescuing Sally.

20

Holding the Bag

by Carolyn Sutton

Kenton's sharp eyes couldn't help noticing a brown lump lying against the curb in front of Mountain View Market. *Must be trash someone threw out their car window,* he mused. *This isn't the best part of town.* Kenton turned his handlebars and leaned hard to the right at the Maple Circle intersection.

A few months before, Kenton had earned the Paper Route Carrier of the Year award. But that honor wasn't warming his icy fingers as the February wind forced its way through his worn-out gloves. His lips felt like ice cubes. With a well-aimed toss, Kenton landed another copy of Thursday's *Union Tribune* on a driveway as he rolled by. *Only two more streets to go,* he thought.

His mother had promised macaroni and cheese for dinner at home. However, the apartment he and his mom had moved into didn't seem like home yet.

What he really couldn't get used to was waking up three mornings a week with his mom gone. He understood that she needed a second job to make ends meet. She'd cried and said she was proud when Kenton told her he'd gotten a paper route to help bring some money to the family. She insisted he save part of it for a computer he'd been wanting. His dad had promised him one, but Kenton saw that promise evaporate when his father walked out of their life.

Something that had not changed since his father's departure was having evening worships with his mom. She always asked him and Brandon how their day had gone. They'd talk about how they'd handled problems during the day. Then his mom would say, "Before we pray, let's talk a minute about how Jesus might have handled that situation."

Kenton finished delivering the Maple Circle papers and turned back onto Mountain View Drive, heading toward the Century Circle intersection. Mountain View Market, and then only five more blocks.

Looking ahead, he noticed the brown object he'd seen earlier. Kenton thought, *It looks bigger than it did before*. The closer he pedaled, the more the "trash" looked like some kind of stuffed bag. Yes—a strange canvas bag, about the size of a large loaf of bread. The icy drizzle around him couldn't dampen Kenton's growing curiosity.

Hopping off his bicycle, he propped it up on the

kickstand and slowly walked along the gutter. The bag was obviously stuffed full of something. Should he risk touching it? Would it explode? Did it contain money?

That last thought did it! Quickly Kenton scooped the muddy bundle out of the gutter. In the headlight beams of an approaching car he could make out the black letters stenciled on the bag: "Mountain View Market." A quick look inside the cover revealed bundles of cash secured by rubber bands. *Someone must've been taking the market's money to the bank and dropped it!* he thought.

With a racing heart Kenton tossed the bag of money into the empty newspaper basket on the rear of his bicycle and started pedaling for home. *There's a lot of money in that bag,* he thought. *Maybe I should keep it. After all, finders keepers—right?* The image of a new computer suddenly rose up out of the mists of his mind.

Then at that exact moment something blindsided Kenton. The words he'd heard his mother speak so often sliced sharply into his conscience: "Let's talk a minute about how Jesus might have handled that situation."

Kenton couldn't escape the obvious answer: keeping money that wasn't his would be dishonest. It was a choice Jesus would never make.

Jesus, he prayed silently, *You know I want to keep this money for a new computer. But most of all, I want to be like You.*

"OK," said Kenton out loud to himself. "If I want to

be like Jesus, my only choice is to return the money."

A few minutes later Kenton placed the soggy canvas sack on the Mountain View Market checkout counter. Almost immediately a total stranger rushed over to hug and kiss him. Someone else pressed a $20 bill into his hand. Obviously, returning the money was making a lot of people very happy.

Later that evening Kenton ate macaroni and cheese while he described to his mother and Brandon what had happened. "The lady who gave me money could've just said 'Thank you.' But," he added with a grin, "it's nice to be $20 closer to a new computer!"

"How much more do you have to save?" Brandon asked.

"Only about $1,000," Kenton said, laughing.

The following afternoon Kenton wheeled his bicycle through the rain into the newspaper dispatch center to pick up his load of papers.

"Look at today's cover story!" the route supervisor said to Kenton when the boy reported for work. As he unrolled one of his papers, Kenton was shocked to see his own face smiling back at him from the front page.

"It tells all about you," the supervisor said. "Even says you've been saving for a computer."

The next week the phone in Kenton's house rang. "Kenton McDougal," a serious-sounding voice said, "we need you and your mother to come down to the *Union Tribune* editor's office at 3:00 today." Kenton called his mother, and she made arrangements to be gone from work.

When they arrived at the newspaper office, five middle-aged men in business suits rose to face Kenton and his mother. A photographer began snapping pictures.

"Kenton," said the newspaper editor, "these businessmen read about the choice you made to be honest, and they want you to know that somehow, in the end, honesty always pays."

One of the businessmen stepped forward. "I'm Mr. Branner," he said, shaking hands with Kenton and his mother. "I'm with Branner Appliances. I read that you're saving for a computer. Here's a check for $200."

"I'm Mr. Hutchins from Central Office Supply," said a shorter man. "Here's another $200 toward your computer."

And so it went down the line, until Kenton was holding checks totaling $1,000.

"By the way," said the editor, who was now smiling broadly, "a lot of readers have been sending in donations for you too. It seems they want you to have a new desk to set your new computer on, along with enough software for you to have everything you need in your homeschool studies. I hope you don't mind being on the front page one more time."

Back in the car, Kenton and his mom leafed through all the checks. A note attached to one of the checks read: "Always keep in mind that you did the right thing." Another note stated: "What you did made my day. I'd kind of given up on kids today. You've helped me believe in them again."

"Mom," Kenton said with a chuckle, "I can't believe I can now get a loaded computer with a printer and a big monitor and a CD-ROM drive—" The boy grew serious. "And to think that all I did was ask Jesus to help me do what He would have done."

The Camel Race

by Patti Emanuele

Ishaya watched as a young scorpion dug deep into the sand. He searched the horizon, shading his eyes with his hand.

"Ishaya, come here and help me with this pot," his mother, Fodora, called to him.

Quickly Ishaya ran to help. The pot was filled with his breakfast—tuo (boiled yam, over which was poured tomato gravy). He dipped a bowl into the pot and began to eat. His friend Tarlift ran up to him.

"Ishaya, come see; the men are coming!"

The boys ran to the edge of the compound. Squinting their eyes against the intense sunlight, they could see a caravan of camels shimmering in the desert heat.

"I hope they traded well," Tarlift said. The men had left one week ago, their camels laden with hand-made leather saddles, silver knives, and jewelry to trade in the ancient city of Erfoud.

The men were closer now. Ishaya could see their colorful robes blowing in the wind as they rode.

Ishaya ran to his father, Garba, and helped unload the leather-wrapped goods he had traded for. Garba gave his son a hearty hug. He had missed his family. His beautiful wife was already unwrapping packages.

Later, after enjoying a refreshing glass of hot mint tea, Garba sat back on his brightly colored rug and spoke to his family of great news.

"Ishaya, I have decided to allow you to run the camels this year," his father told him.

Every year his family traveled to the Cure Salee, or "salt cure," where exhausted herds are restored with large amounts of salt. The Wodaabe and Tuareg peoples would gather there for a festival. For the Tuaregs, it was a time for "tindes," or camel dances and races. Only men were allowed to compete in the races.

Later, alone in their shelter, Garba spoke to his wife and son.

"Ishaya, you will compete, but you must not race in the former way," he whispered to them both.

Outside, a cold chill swept across the desert as nighttime fell. Ishaya pulled his robe closer around his body.

"Yes, Ishaya," his mother agreed with her husband. "We must do as Jesus would have us do."

It had been many days since the Christian people

had lived among them. Fodora, always curious, had asked one of them, Maryanna, why she did not say the usual ritual prayers.

"I believe that Jesus Christ is the only way to God" had been her reply. Her love for Fodora and her people had convinced the Tuareg woman that she also wanted to believe. Later, her husband had also followed this Jesus.

To their friends and family, nothing seemed to change. The women of the family still packed up the shelter, cooking utensils, and meager belongings to follow the ancient trade routes in search of a good supply of water. Everything they owned was loaded onto camels, and their small herds of goats and cows followed behind.

Since Ishaya was the oldest son, his job was to watch over the sheep herds. He made certain they received enough water. He had even helped birth a baby goat.

"Ishaya, isn't this great? We're going to race the camels this year!" his best friend, Hussein, said to him.

It was exciting, but Ishaya was worried. It was not unheard of in the heat of the competition for a camel to suddenly become injured, a leather saddle to be missing, or even a contestant not to wake up from his sleep.

When he arrived in Merzouga, it was everything Ishaya had remembered. He could smell goat roasting on the fire, hear women laughing and singing, and watch men greeting old friends.

On the third day Ishaya joined his father and friends as they discussed race tactics under the shade of a palm tree. Later, as he dressed, he overheard some of the other boys talking about the race.

"If we win, we will have much girma," said one.

"The prize is a purse of silver coins," said another.

Ishaya watched as they fingered their tcherot, a small silver box containing select verses from their holy book. Since becoming a Christian, Ishaya wore no tcherot. He had memorized some words from a Bible that the Christians had shared with his family. To follow Jesus meant he was different from his friends and could even mean banishment from his group.

"There is a book spoken from Jesus to our people," Garba had shared one day. "I know where to get one, but I would have to trade something very valuable to get it."

Ishaya wanted to learn more about Jesus. Instinctively he knew that he would have to trust God to win the race. He would give the prize to his father, and together they would find the merchant who held the book.

Later that morning Garba approached his son. "Ishaya, I was sick last night. I won't be able to race today. Now it is up to you to capture the prize for us."

As the boys mounted their camels, Ishaya whispered, "O God, help me to do this for You."

Shouts filled the air as the camels awkwardly

struggled to their feet. Ishaya carefully watched the two riders on either side of him.

Muhammed leaned forward on his camel. From behind his veil, dark eyes shone with hatred. "Do not even bother to mount," he said to Ishaya. "Even your new faith will not protect you. Your camel may 'suddenly' trip and fall."

Ishaya heard the laughter of the rider on his other side. He was a burly man, an experienced rider. "Ride and learn," he hissed at the young rider.

Ishaya remembered his father's warning: "They will seek to win at any cost, my son. Be careful."

At the sound of the ram's horn, they were off. Ishaya urged his camel forward. Awakened from its trance, the beast began to gallop. Riders on either side of him shouted at their animals. Ishaya struggled to remain in control of his beast as the rider next to him drove his camel into his side. The big animal faltered, then picked up speed. Ishaya tensed on his reins as he felt the animal stumble, then gain control.

Ishaya was in the lead now, but riders gained on him. Dust swirled around his face. He could feel his camel laboring to run, its sides heaving and its breath coming in short gasps.

Without looking, Ishaya sensed another rider gaining on him. He turned and stared into the dark eyes of his competitor. He was smiling oddly at Ishaya as he raised his arm above his head.

The man's riding stick struck Ishaya sharply on the leg. The opponent's animal then bolted forward into the lead. Ishaya's own riding stick hung at his side. Fighting the urge to strike back, Ishaya chose not to use it.

Instead, Ishaya dug deeper into the sides of his beast. Frothy saliva fell from the camel's mouth and splattered against Ishaya's dark robe. The young rider's eyes burned with desire for the goal that was now within his sight.

Ahead of him a red banner stretched across the blowing sand. Crowds of onlookers shouted at them. Children jumped up and down. Ishaya was so close, and his heart began to pound.

He pulled even with the lead rider. Suddenly the man turned once more and began beating Ishaya with his stick. Angrily the camel turned and bared its teeth at its abuser. The man, swaying atop his galloping mount, missed Ishaya with one large stroke and struck Ishaya's camel. The animal, incensed and in pain, lurched forward and pulled Ishaya across the finish line.

Grasping the leather pouch containing his prize, Ishaya raised it above his head for all to see. "This prize belongs to Jesus!" he cried out.

And the Book would soon belong to Ishaya and his family.

22

"The Basket Is Very High"

as told to Patricia Karwatowicz

My great-uncle Adam is history in a nutshell. He was born in Poland 85 years ago, and the weird thing is he likes me. It turns out he's dying to come to one of my basketball games, even though he's never seen a live basketball game in his life! He even asked me, "How high is the basket for throwing in the ball?"

What would the other Hornets say if my great-uncle came to a game in his goofy fur-flapped hat, long overcoat, and galoshes? The guys would make hay out of that. (Oh, no! I'm beginning to talk like him.)

It's doubly weird because my parents named me after him, saying my uncle is a very honorable man. My great-aunt Margaret calls him "Big Adam" and me "Young Adam" to tell us apart. I can almost hear someone calling me "Young Adam" in public.

My problem is that I'm required to spend "quality time" with Great-uncle and Great-aunt Karwatowicz. Dad says it's so they won't get lonely. Mom says it's a good experience. Mostly I call my visit a school service project. But I know it's important to make sure they're OK.

Uncle is crazy about stamp collecting. For years he's been buying mint-condition stamps from stamp stores and post offices around the world. He has tons and tons of albums, but he can't see very well and needs my help mounting his latest purchases in the albums.

I have to admit we've had some fun conversations, dreaming about how someday he'll sell a really valuable one and imagining what he'll do with the money. He'd like to go back to Poland and see his farm that got confiscated during the war, then slip into his old Krakow church, and after that maybe buy a paczki. Uncle says to pronounce it "poonch-key"— a jelly-filled doughnut.

The morning for my next visit comes around, and Uncle opens their condo door. "Come in, Ah-dem!"

"Is that Young Adam?" calls Aunt Margaret. "Have a spot of tea, dear." Just so you know, that doesn't mean a drip of tea on your shirt; it's Aunt M's British-speak for "a cup of tea."

"Two lumps of sugar or three?" She spoons spearmint leaves into the flowered teapot and pours boiling water into it. Then—get this—she puts a little sweater thing over the pot to keep it hot. Aunt M calls it "a cozy."

"Two lumps, please," I answer politely. Aunt M is big on politeness.

I'm not exactly into tea, but it's a good way to kill time, so I have some. The homemade shortbread isn't a problem. The three of us sit at the table with a centerpiece of medicine bottles. A few breakfast crumbs, too. My "greats" can't see very well.

"How are you today, Uncle?"

"I'm a little veak." Uncle slurps his tea, then scoots his chair back from the table. "Vell? Ready for some stamping, Ah-dem?"

"Sure." I wipe buttery crumbs from my lips with a cloth napkin. Aunt M isn't into paper napkins.

She squints at me. "Perhaps you'd prefer to play a game? My lady friends will be coming down soon. We could use a fourth player."

"Thanks for the tea, Aunt Margaret, but Uncle asked first." Whew.

Uncle shuffles in his purple bedroom slippers to the dining room. A fat album lies open on the table under a large magnifying glass. He hands me some special stamp tweezers. "Remember, no fingerprints on our stamps. Ve must keep them impeccable to remain valuable."

"Right."

I mount his latest art series on the page. Uncle settles back to watch. "Someday ve vill find a very rare stamp, Ah-dem."

"Right. What will our $100,000 stamp buy this time?"

"It is not impossible. If a stamp has an error—for example, something is upside down—they stop the printing and it becomes rare." He leans back thoughtfully in his chair. "Ve vould buy the farm I lost in the var . . ."

"Tell me more, Uncle."

"Ve had no baskets for the ball there. Only baskets for gathering eggs." He chuckles. "Ve had fields to plow behind the horse, and a varm fire, and ve had time to thank the Lord. Ah-dem, do you have time to thank the Lord?"

I haven't been doing much thanking the Lord lately, I realize. *Maybe I'd better do something positive, such as a good deed.* "Uncle, if you want, you can watch my basketball game tomorrow."

"How you say? Right!"

I tell Dad and Mom I finally invited Great-uncle Adam to a game. They smile, so I know I'm in the right court, so to speak.

The next day during pregame warm-ups I hear guffaws and snorts from my teammates. "Who's that ol' geezer?" "Totally weird!" "He's older'n dirt!"

Great-uncle Adam shuffles onto the gym floor

tapping his cane, leaning on Dad's arm. Uncle sees me right off and calls, "Hullo! Hullo, Young Ah-dem!"

Eric asks, "He belongs to you?"

"Nah," I answer. "He's just some old guy my parents know."

Nice going, Adam, I think. *Real honorable*.

The game is close. In the last seconds the Hornets are down two points—ball in my hands, I position myself for a three-pointer, the shot I never miss. Dead silence. Then a shout: "Make the ball in the basket, Young Ah-dem!"

I miss. The winners cheer. The Hornets moan. After high-fiving the victors, I slink off the court, mad and embarrassed—big-time. So much for my good deed.

Eric taunts, "Young Ahhh-dem, who's that old guy who threw you off your shot?"

Jim asks, "Yeah, he looked like a major time warp."

Noah doesn't say anything.

Then I get as mad as a hornet! It's my great-uncle they're talking about. I invited Uncle so he could see me play, not so he could be seen and ridiculed. I have to stand up for him.

"He's my great-uncle Adam. I'm named after him. Uncle is a decorated Polish war hero who immigrated to this country 50 years ago with nothing but the clothes on his back. He's an expert stamp collector, too. We can't pick our relatives, but if I could, I'd pick him."

Eric shrugs. Jim says, "Whatever." And good ol' Noah says, "That was cool, man."

I march off with a bounce in my sneakers and climb into the backseat of the car next to my great-uncle Adam.

Dad says, "We can't win 'em all."

Mom says, "It's only a game."

Uncle Adam says, "But the basket is very high." He touches my hand with his very old hand. "Ve may have lost the war, Ah-dem, but always there is another field to plow. Ve thank the Lord for that."

I look into his warm, blue eyes and thank the Lord for my great-uncle Adam. "What do you say, Uncle? Let's go home and light that warm fire and find that valuable stamp."

"Vell, I think that is a good idea, Ah-dem."

23

Hans-Josef's Heroic Day

by Elfriede Volk

Sixteen-year-old Hans-Josef trudged slowly over the cobblestones that paved the streets of Rotterdam's main harbor. His eyes were down, as was his mood.

World War II had just ended, and Hans-Josef and his mother had come to the Netherlands from Germany to start their lives over again. For two hours the teen had used up good shoe leather visiting the businesses in the area, trying to get a job. The people had just laughed at him.

"You?" they had asked. "What makes you think we'd want to hire you? You're a German, aren't you? Well, we had enough of them when they occupied our land."

He had tried to explain that he was only part German, that his father had been Dutch, but they wouldn't listen.

"Go back to where you came from. We don't want you here."

A few had been kinder, but their remarks had hurt just as much.

"With all the men who have returned from the war, you don't stand a chance of getting a job. You're just a kid. You have no experience. What could you possibly do?"

Hans-Josef clenched his hands together in his pockets, hard, so that the nails dug in. The pain helped him to focus and keep from crying. Seeing a pebble on the road, he kicked it and sent it bouncing over the cobbles.

What could he do? He could play soccer and swim and march, but his Hitler Youth training had not prepared him for much else. There certainly had not been any chance to start an apprenticeship. And without a father to make arrangements for him now, it was doubtful if he would ever get one.

He passed Emergency Housing, surrounded by mountains of rubble from the buildings and machinery that had been destroyed in the bombing. Emergency Housing was home now, but he did not want to go there. Not yet. He did not want to let his mother know that he had again failed to find a job. Instead, he walked to the end of the Wilhelminakade, where stood the head office of the Holland America Line, a transatlantic shipping company. There was a tiny patch of grass in front of the building, and he hoped he could sit there to think about what he should do next.

The pier was deserted, except for two preschool children playing in a pile of sand that had been dredged from the bottom of the harbor. Hans-Josef recognized them from Emergency Housing. They were engrossed in their game and did not see him as he stretched out on the grass. The sod beneath him felt cool, the sun overhead warm. The buzzing of insects made him drowsy, and, putting his head on his arms, he dozed off.

Minutes or hours later, he woke with a start and sat up. The girl was no longer there, but the boy was still at the end of the pier, motionless, staring down into the water. Hans-Josef stood up and brushed the dirt off his pants. Then, curious, he walked over to where the boy stood.

"What's so inter—" he began.

The boy looked at him, wide-eyed, then ran off screaming.

"Strange," Hans-Josef said to himself, shaking his head. "Very strange." Except for a large piece of wood, he could see nothing in the water. "That kid's going to have problems when he—"

He was just turning away when he saw it. A small bare foot came up out of the water, then went down again. He had a sickening feeling as he recalled a similar experience from the past, but the other time the person in trouble had been an adult at a public beach. Now it was a child, and he was alone, with no one to help him.

Tearing off his jacket and taking a deep breath, he dived down to where he had seen the foot disappear.

The water was shockingly cold and dirty, bearing silt from spring runoff. The grit ground against his eyes, but he forced himself to keep them open so he could see. His wet clothes clung to him, making swimming difficult, and his lungs felt as if they would explode. Yet he forced himself to go deeper, feeling, searching, praying.

Finally, when he felt he could not stay submerged any longer, his fingers snagged some material and clenched around it. He popped to the surface, dragging a limp body with him. It was the little girl he had seen earlier, but now her eyes were closed, her face colorless. Tears mingled with the water dripping down his face as he held her in one arm and clambered up the embankment.

Reaching the top, Hans-Josef laid the girl facedown on the cobblestones, then pressed gently on her back. Water gushed from her nose and mouth. "Oh, God," he prayed, "don't let it be too late! Don't let her die."

He alternated pressing on the tot's back and lifting her arms and shoulders to get air into her lungs.

"Here," a voice said behind him. "Wrap yourself in this blanket so you won't get sick, and let me take over."

Hans-Josef looked up to see that the pier was no longer deserted. A crowd of people had gathered out of nowhere, among them a medical officer from the Holland America Line. He let the man take over.

About a month later reporters gathered in the main hall of the Emergency Housing building. A government official hung a medal around Hans-Josef's neck, and the reporters snapped several pictures of the teen and the tot he had saved.

"Did you see her fall into the water?" one reporter asked.

"No, I was asleep."

"Then how did you . . . ?"

"I just woke up suddenly, saw this boy looking into the water, and when I went over—"

"Did he wake you?"

"No."

"Then who . . . ? How . . . ?"

"I don't know. I don't know who or what woke me. I just woke up and saw her foot, then jumped in."

Hans-Josef may not have known who woke him, but I am convinced that it was my guardian angel. You see, I am the little girl he saved that day, and I am looking forward to seeing and thanking both Hans-Josef and my angel.

24

The Big Oops

by Karen Troncale

At my school kids had no respect for one another. If they heard something that someone didn't want people to know, they'd tell everyone. I worried they'd find out about my ugly little secret.

But I'm ashamed to say that I used to talk about other kids, too. Why? Because that's what everybody did.

Until Julia showed up.

Julia arrived at our school toward the end of fifth grade. I liked her from the first day I met her. There really wasn't anything about her not to like. She wasn't exactly pretty, but she was kind of cute. She already knew a lot of the school stuff we were working on, so she was pretty smart. And Julia was a terrific dresser. Every outfit looked great on her. She always wore something special—a long scarf tied around her waist, an unusual vest, or some other unique accessory.

Julia and I talked together in class and helped each other with homework during recess. One day she invited me to her house after school. I told her I'd ask my mom at lunch, since I lived around the corner from the school and always went home to eat.

"What did your mom say?" she asked when she saw me later.

I gave her the thumbs-up signal.

"Great! I'll meet you at your locker after school."

The last bell rang. I walked past the girls' restroom on the way to my locker. I paused for a second. I needed to use it, but I hated to go in there. It was always filthy. I don't know why some girls thought it was funny to trash up the bathrooms. So I walked on by.

"Let's go!" said Julia.

"Is your house very far?" I asked.

"No, it's not far at all," she replied.

That was the day I learned that not everyone sees things the same way. To me a house that was "not far at all" was like my house—right around the corner. To Julia a house that was several long blocks away was "not far at all" because she had once lived in a house that was more than a mile away from her school.

The afternoon sun beat down on us as we walked and talked. "Where do you get your clothes?" I asked. "You always look great."

"At the thrift store," she answered, as though there was nothing wrong with it.

Oh, no, I thought. *If the kids at school find out she wears used clothing, they'll really tease her.* I wanted to tell her to never mention that to anyone else, but I didn't.

Soon I began to wish I'd used the girls' bathroom. I really had to go. Every time we came to another street, I hoped it was Julia's. But we kept walking and walking. I became more and more uncomfortable. I had to get to a bathroom soon!

Finally she turned down a side street. "Is this your street?" I asked hopefully.

"That's my house," she said, pointing. "Dad must not be home yet. I don't see his car."

I hurried toward the door. But Julia called out, "It'll be locked. We'll have to wait in the backyard." She walked to a side gate.

Oh, no! I had to get in now!

I followed her to the backyard. "This happens a lot," Julia said. "Dad tries to be here when I get home, but he's a youth pastor and has a lot to do. So sometimes he's late. He'll be here soon." She kicked off her shoes and picked up the end of a hose. "It sure is hot! Let's cool off our feet." She turned on the water.

That did it. I couldn't hold it any longer. A warm, wet trickle ran down my pant legs. A wet stain spread out across the patio cement.

I turned bright red. This couldn't be happening to me! Girls my age did not wet their pants! I wanted the ground to open up and swallow me so I could disappear. I scrunched up my face and tried not to cry.

Julia's eyes grew big. She looked at the stain and back up at me. Her hand flew up to her mouth. "Oh, my!" she said. Then suddenly she turned the hose on herself. Soon she was dripping with water.

"Your turn!" she said, pointing the hose at me. She sprayed me until I was soaking wet, and then she sprayed off the sidewalk, too.

Just then a car pulled into the driveway. Her dad went through the house and unlocked the back door.

"I'm sorry I wasn't here when you got home," he said to Julia. "Hey, that's a great way to cool off!" He pointed to our wet clothes.

"Dad, this is my friend Karen," said Julia.

"I'm glad to meet you," he said, smiling.

I don't remember much of what happened the rest of the afternoon. I know Julia let me borrow some of her dry clothes, and later her dad drove me home. I went straight to my room. I didn't want to see anyone.

I thought about what I'd done. When the kids at school found out, I'd be laughed at forever. I could never go to school again.

But of course I couldn't stay home. So the next day I went to school. When I saw Julia in class, my face turned pink. However, she acted happy to see me. The rest of the day I watched her. Every time she talked to someone I wondered if she was telling them what I did.

The day finally ended. But the next day was worse. Desiree was having a sleepover. I wasn't invited, because Desiree and I weren't good friends. What worried me was that she'd invited Julia. I knew what happened at sleepovers. Kids talked about other kids. Julia would talk about me. She'd tell them what had happened. What was I going to do?

By Monday I was a nervous wreck. I walked slowly into class. I felt as if I were wearing a big sign that read "I WET MY PANTS." But Julia just smiled when I walked in. Nobody looked at me funny. And nothing happened the rest of the day. I realized that Julia hadn't said anything to anyone. I was safe!

By the end of the year Julia was one of my best friends. She never, ever mentioned what had happened, even to me. When she discovered that my family didn't go to a church, she invited me to hers. I began to learn about Jesus.

Before school started again in September, Julia's dad got transferred to another church. After they moved, I never saw her again. But I never forgot her. Much later I realized that Julia was living her life the way Jesus wanted her to—by being kind and good.

Now I try to be like her. I don't talk about other people if I hear about something dumb that they said or did. Because I know what I would have felt like if Julia had told people what I'd done.

I don't want anybody to feel like that. Ever.